VEGAN COOKING

The Compassionate Way of Eating

by

LEAH LENEMAN

Illustrated by Ivana T. Cooke

A THORSONS COOKBOOK
WHOLEFOOD

THORSONS PUBLISHERS LIMITED
Wellingborough, Northamptonshire

First published 1982
Fifth Impression 1985

British Library Cataloguing in Publication Data

Leneman, Leah
    Vegan cooking.
    1. Vegetarian cookery.
    I. Title
    641.5'636   TX837

    ISBN 0-7225-0753-4

Printed in Great Britain by
Richard Clay (The Chaucer Press) Ltd,
Bungay, Suffolk

VEGAN COOKING

Variety is the key-note of this book which proves that vegan recipes can be nourishing, colourful and quick to prepare.

CONTENTS

PUBLISHER'S NOTE

Where recipes call for the inclusion of margarine this has been listed as polyunsaturated margarine, but since some polyunsaturated margarines are not vegan it is recommended that readers use the known vegan margarine which they are most used to.

INTRODUCTION

Vegetarianism is entering a new and dynamic phase. A cuisine based on vegetables, fruits, nuts and grains, flavoured with all of the herbs and spices of the world, is taking the place of a diet reliant on dairy produce. This has come about firstly because of the growing realization that everyone in the world could be fed if a switch were made to a completely vegetarian diet. Britain could be self-sufficient if grazing lands were used to grow *legumes* and grains were fed direct to humans instead of being diverted to animals. Since dairy farming is almost as inefficient a way of using land as beef farming, the switch must be complete, if it is to be effective.

It is not only human beings who would benefit, for slaughter-houses would disappear. Lacto-vegetarians are beginning to realize that drinking cows' milk contributes to animal slaughter. Cows are kept continually pregnant and lactating, their calves usually taken away very shortly after birth (many ending their brief lives as veal), so that the milk can all go for human consumption. Even if factory farming were to be abolished, male calves would still have to be slaughtered to maintain the dairy industry. Similarly, in order to get laying hens there have to be fertile eggs, and all of the male chicks will be killed. Thus, while free-ranging hens do not have to endure the inhumane battery system, eating any kind of eggs still contributes to animal slaughter.

There are so many second, third and even fourth generation lacto-vegetarians in this country now that no one could convincingly claim that flesh foods are necessary for health. Many people still fear, however, that to give up all animal produce is dangerous (and anyone who embarks on a vegan diet whilst riddled with apprehensions may well become ill from sheer anxiety). In fact, many lacto-vegetarians consume an excessive amount of dairy produce, thereby clogging up their arteries with saturated fat – a far greater health risk than a vegan diet.

The biggest worry is protein. Giving up cheese and eggs, it is felt, will mean eating only 'inferior', and therefore insufficient, protein. Fortunately it has become more generally known that one can combine cereals with *légumes* or nuts to obtain all the necessary amino acids (the building blocks of protein) in required proportions. This combination forms the basis of many of the recipes in this book, so that it would be virtually impossible for anyone using it to become deficient in protein. It is certainly not necessary to eat foods high in protein at every meal.

The one and only nutrient which does not occur naturally in a vegan diet is vitamin B_{12}. Although some pioneering vegans who had never heard of this vitamin appear to have been able to synthesize it in their intestines, the effects of a deficiency are too drastic to make it worth the risk. Most of the plant milks now available in Britain are fortified with vitamin B_{12}, and so are most textured vegetable protein (t.v.p.) products. There are a number of other foods also fortified with B_{12}, including *Tastex* and *Barmene* yeast extracts, and *Grapenuts* cereal. As only a small amount of this vitamin is required, it is very easy to incorporate it into a vegan diet by eating any of the above foods regularly. For those who prefer not to use any processed foods, there are vegan vitamin B_{12} tablets available in health food stores.

Some vegans limit their use of sugar, both because of its lack of nutritional content and because many sugars have been refined using charcoal from animal bones; this is one of those instances where individual consciences differ. Honey is a much more contentious issue as, strictly speaking, it is an animal product, though its use should not cause suffering. The question has been debated over the years and vegans generally have agreed to differ. Although a substantial number of vegans do use honey, in fairness to those who do not, honey is not used in any of the recipes in this book.

The concern with animal exploitation which causes people to give up eating animal products usually spills over into other areas as well. Most vegans would not wear leather or use soaps or cosmetics containing animal products, though once again individual consciences vary. Wool and lanolin are more marginal issues, though on purely aesthetic grounds the idea of putting sheep fat on one's face can be off-putting.

Some vegetarians who are vegan at home find it difficult to maintain this diet elsewhere. This is understandable in view of British restaurants' obsession with animal produce, but it is possible to get delicious vegan meals in many Indian and Chinese restaurants, and any good Italian restaurant can prepare pizzas without cheese.

Vegans have varied eating patterns. There are those who eat only raw foods, those who stick strictly to unprocessed wholefoods, and others who rely mainly on t.v.p. and vegan convenience meals. Variety is the key-note of this book. The philosophy here is that if the basic diet is one of natural unrefined foods, then there is no harm at all in utilizing a certain amount of good quality processed and packaged foods to add different tastes and textures, as well as to save time.

Vegan cookery can be as quick as any other kind. After all, one of the most popular foods in Britain is baked beans on toast – a quick and nutritious vegan snack, particularly if the bread is wholemeal. A number of the recipes in this book can be prepared in half an hour or less. It is simply a question of gearing oneself to the use of a completely different set of foods; once that becomes ingrained then no great mental effort is required to prepare quick-and-easy healthy meals. And should any still think that vegan food lacks variety, this book will prove just how wrong they are.

Note: For more detailed information on both the ethical and nutritional aspects of a vegan diet, please contact The Vegan Society, 47 Highlands Road, Leatherhead, Surrey KT22 8NQ.

GENERAL NOTES

- All recipes are meant to serve four, though individual appetites naturally vary a good deal.

- Proprietary brand names are mentioned only if there is no vegan alternative – e.g. *Sun-O-Life* dressing, *Morga* vegetable stock cubes, Barbara's Organic Mashed Potatoes, etc.

- Quantities for herbs always refer to the dried variety, so amounts should be adjusted accordingly if using fresh herbs.

- When referring to a quantity of wholemeal pastry – e.g. ½ lb (¼ kilo) the weight of the flour rather than the total weight is meant. To make successful wholemeal pastry, use finely ground wholemeal flour, half as much polyunsaturated margarine or vegetable fat (e.g. *Trex*) as flour, and a little sea salt. Rub the fat into the flour, then add enough water to make a dough. The secret to making a light wholemeal pastry is first, to have a moist soft dough (the board should be well floured to avoid sticking), and second, to avoid handling the dough any more than is absolutely necessary. To make a pre-baked pie shell follow the above instructions, roll out the dough thinly, place in a greased tart tin, and prick in various spots with a fork. Bake in a hot oven at 425°F/220°C (Gas Mark 7) for 10 minutes and then for about 20 minutes, or until done, in a moderate oven at 350°F/180°C (Gas Mark 4).

1.
THE VEGAN DAIRY

Milk
At the time of writing there are five soya milks available through health food stores.

1. *Plamil Soya Plant Milk* (Plamil Foods Ltd.) – made by the only ethically vegan firm in Britain, this is a highly nutritious milk, available either in tetrapack cartons or tins. The distinctive flavour may take some getting used to, but it has achieved wide popularity. Fortified with vitamin B_{12}.

2. *Golden Archer Soya Plant Milk* (Itona Products Ltd.) – another British soya milk, this one is made from soya flour and is available in tinned form. Does not contain B_{12}.

3. *Granogen* (Granose Foods Ltd.) – made in the U.S.A. As this is a powdered soya milk, added to liquid as required, the keeping qualities are obviously better than tinned varieties which must be used fairly quickly after opening. It has a sweet, slightly malted flavour and is fortified with B_{12}. (*Granolac* is a powdered soya milk specially formulated for infants.)

4. *Soyvita* (Healtheries Ltd.) – another powdered soya milk, this time from New Zealand. It may be too sweet for some tastes but would suit those who are not keen on a pronounced 'soya' flavour. Fortified with B_{12}.

5. *Liquid Soya Milk* (Granose Foods Ltd.) – this comes in a carton like dairy milk. The flavour is perhaps the most generally acceptable and purists might prefer it for its simpler formulation. It is not, however, fortified with B_{12}.

6. *Provamel Soya Drink* – another very pleasant liquid milk in a carton; it comes from Belgium. Not fortified with B_{12}.

HOME-MADE SOYA MILK

1. Bring about 1 pint (½ litre) of water to the boil, add 4 oz (100g) soya beans, boil for 1 minute, then remove from the heat, cover and leave to soak overnight.

2. Drain the beans and wash them thoroughly. Put 1 cupful of beans in a liquidizer, add about 1 pint (½ litre) hot water and blend them thoroughly. Pour through a clean tea-towel or cheese-cloth, squeezing to extract all the liquid (the pulp can be used for savoury dishes, if desired). Repeat until all the beans are used up.

3. Bring the milk to the boil, stirring frequently. (It has a tendency both to burn on the bottom of the pan and to boil over if not watched carefully!)

4. Simmer the milk over the lowest possible heat for 15-20 minutes. Set aside to cool and then keep in the fridge.

5. This can be made more palatable by adding pure vanilla essence or sweetening to taste.

A very pleasant milk can be made from cashew nuts as follows:

CASHEW NUT MILK

4 oz (100g) cashew nuts
½ pint (¼ litre) water
Raw cane sugar or chopped dates to taste
1 dessertspoonful vegetable oil

1. Put the cashews into the liquidizer and grind finely. Add the other ingredients and liquidize thoroughly.

Note: This can be made thicker or thinner, if preferred, by increasing or decreasing the proportion of nuts and oil to water.

ALMOND MILK

Using the same quantity of blanched almonds, proceed as above. Delicious but expensive.

Note: For tea and coffee there is a vegan equivalent of Coffee-Mate called *Pareve-Mate* (distributed by Eliko Food Distributors Ltd., Unit D, Ashley Works, Ashley Road, London N17 9LJ).

Cream

Delice (Plamil Foods Ltd.) – those who like *Plamil* will find this very useful as it is the only ready-made nutritious vegan cream on the market. It does, however, have a strong flavour which may not appeal to all palates.

Granogen (see the section on milk) – can be made up using a higher proportion of powder to water to produce a thick cream.

The following recipes use *Granogen* to make a whipped cream:

SOYA WHIPPED CREAM I

⅓ pint (200 ml) water
4 oz (100g) Granogen
4 fl oz (100 ml) vegetable oil
½ teaspoonful pure vanilla essence
Squeeze of lemon juice

1. Add the powder to the water in a liquidizer. Add the vanilla essence, and then add the oil slowly, liquidizing between additions. Finally add the lemon juice, liquidize one last time and chill.

SOYA WHIPPED CREAM II

½ pint (¼ litre) water
2 oz (50g) polyunsaturated margarine
4 oz (100g) Granogen
Raw cane sugar to taste
1 teaspoonful agar-agar

1. Liquidize the water and the Granogen. Pour the mixture into a saucepan and bring to the boil.

2. Add the agar-agar to the milk and simmer for a minute or two.

3. Place the margarine in a liquidizer. Pour the milk in and blend thoroughly, adding sweetening to taste.

4. Pour into a bowl and chill in the fridge. When chilled, beat with an egg-whisk to the consistency of whipped cream. (Proportions of the ingredients may be varied to make the cream thicker or thinner, richer or less rich).

The following is particularly useful for shortcakes or trifle:

MOCK CREAM

1-2 tablespoonsful cornflour
½pint (¼ litre) any soya milk
1-2oz (25-50g) polyunsaturated margarine
1oz (25g) raw cane sugar (*not* Demerara)

1. Blend the cornflour to a smooth mixture with a little of the soya milk, then add the rest of the milk; pour the mixture into a saucepan and bring slowly to the boil, stirring constantly. Cook until thickened, then remove from the heat and set aside to cool.

2. Cream the margarine and sugar until very soft, but on no account warm the margarine.

3. Gradually beat in spoonsful of the cornflour mixture – the more you beat this, the better it becomes.

Cashew nuts also make a very palatable cream:

CASHEW NUT CREAM

4 oz (100g) cashew nuts
¼ pint (150ml) water
1 tablespoonful vegetable oil
Raw cane sugar or chopped dates to taste
1 teaspoonful pure vanilla essence (optional)

1. Grind the cashews finely in a liquidizer. Add the rest of the
    ingredients and liquidize thoroughly.

Note: Thickness or thinness of the cream may be adjusted
according to taste by altering the proportion of cashews and oil
to water.

Finally, there are imitation creams such as Snowcrest Imitation
Cream, available through Jewish speciality shops and delicatessens. (Sainsbury's imitation cream is similar, but Sainsbury's are
unable to confirm that the emulsifier used is always of vegetable
origin.) These imitation creams have no nutritional content to
speak of, but they have no intrusive flavour either and so are
perhaps more generally acceptable to non-vegans. It is possible
to make an imitation cream at home with a product called Edifas A
(obtainable from Bow Produce Ltd., 25 Burdon Lane, Cheam,
Surrey). *Note:* The instructions state that the cream should be
used as soon as possible after making, but in fact, if made at
home, it really must be used immediately as it lacks an
emulsifier. Once again, this is low in nutritional content, but
would be free of preservatives and other additives.

VANILLA ICE CREAM

½ pint (¼ litre) water
4 oz (100g) Granogen
1 dessertspoonful pure vanilla essence
Raw cane sugar or chopped dates to taste
4 tablespoonsful vegetable oil

1. Liquidize all the ingredients. Place in the freezer compartment of the fridge at the lowest setting.

2. After an hour or two, put the mixture back through the liquidizer again. It may then be eaten as a soft ice cream. Alternatively, put it back in the freezer but at a higher setting. If, when due to be served, the ice cream is too hard, then remove it from the freezer compartment and place it in the fridge for about 15-20 minutes.

For other ice cream recipes see pp.118, 120 and 121.

COCONUT CREAM

2-4 oz (25-50g) creamed coconut
¼ pint (150ml) very hot water (or to taste)
Sweetening to taste

1. Grate the creamed coconut into a liquidizer or jar. Add the hot water and sweetening, liquidize or shake until the coconut has completely dissolved. Chill in fridge. This can be made as a pouring cream or as a thick cream of a clotted cream texture. It will thicken up when chilled so always make it a bit thinner than desired.

Note: This makes a particularly good topping for fresh strawberries or raspberries.

Yogurt

Commercially dried yogurt cultures used for fermenting dairy milk work equally well on soya milk. Follow the basic instructions on the packet (available at any health food store), but note that it is essential to boil the soya milk before cooling it to lukewarm. An inexpensive wide-mouthed thermos flask will do just as well as a yogurt maker. The initial two or three batches will be rather liquid and sweet, but after that one can get a thick, rich, creamy, rather tart yogurt. After the initial batch, a spoonful of home-made soya yogurt is all that is needed as a starter and, if a small quantity is made frequently, it is possible to keep going for many months without having to buy any more of the commercial starter. Soya yogurt can be used exactly as dairy yogurt. A quick and simple dessert can be made by adding fresh fruit or some spoonsful of raw sugar jam. Vegans who suffer from poor digestion and wind will find that soya yogurt works wonders.

Note: As the bacteria which make the yogurt ferments will have been cultivated in dairy milk, the initial batch of soya yogurt may not be strictly vegan; however, all subsequent batches will be.

Margarine

Most of the soft, so-called 'vegetable' margarines on the market contain whey and/or milk powder, and are therefore not vegan. On the other hand, many proprietary slimmers' spreads (e.g. *Safeway, Co-op*) are completely vegan. These are very handy for spreading on bread, and it does no harm to halve one's calorific intake of margarine for spreading. They cannot, however, be used for cooking. *Tomor* kosher margarine may be the most readily available of vegan margarines. It has a texture similar to that of butter – i.e. hard when cold, soft when warm – but can be left unrefrigerated without 'going off'. The only similar margarine is *Golden Rose* from Belgium, but that is not easily obtainable. There is also a *Golden Rose* diet spread which has a high nutritional content and a delicious flavour, but it is expensive. *Telma* make a soft vegan margarine available at some Jewish delicatessens. The latest vegan margarine to appear in health food stores is *Vitaquell*. It is a high quality soft margarine made from cold-pressed oils; very nutritious and also quite expensive.

Cheese

The following is a good substitute for hard cheese:

SOYA FLOUR CHEESE

Equal quantities of soya flour and polyunsaturated margarine
Yeast extract to taste

1. Melt the margarine, add the soya flour and yeast extract and mix well.

2. Pour onto a greased tin and refrigerate until required. If a soft margarine is used then the resulting 'cheese' is easy to spread. If *Tomor* margarine is used then the 'cheese' can be sliced for sandwiches or grated and sprinkled over a hot savoury to be grilled or baked.

The following is like a soft cheese spread, handy for biscuits, baked potatoes etc.

PIMENTO 'CHEESE' SPREAD

4 oz (100g) cashew nuts
1 small tin pimentos
1 tablespoonful sesame seeds
1 teaspoonful brewer's yeast (optional)
½ teaspoonful onion salt
4 tablespoonsful vegetable oil
2 teaspoonsful lemon juice

1. Grind the cashews and sesame seeds finely.

2. Add the tin of pimentos (including the juice) and the rest of the ingredients. Liquidize thoroughly.

YOGURT CHEESE

Place some thick soya yogurt in a cheese-cloth and tie securely; hang the cheese-cloth over a tap to drip for several hours or overnight, then refrigerate. This is a soft cheese similar to a cream cheese in texture.

CASHEW COTTAGE CHEESE

Cover some cashew nuts with lukewarm water. Leave undisturbed in a warm spot for three or four days. Drain off the liquid and grind the fermented cashews in a Mouli or grinder. (A liquidizer can be used, but the texture will be different.) Use with salads, particularly those with fruit.

For Cheesecake recipes see pp. 32 and 33.

Eggs

Egg substitutes made from arrowroot and other vegan ingredients are readily available in U.S. health food stores. With the steadily increasing number of American products being imported, it is possible that they will soon become available in Britain. As will become apparent from the recipes in this book, an egg substitute is not at all necessary in vegan cookery; it is merely handy if one has a favourite recipe which includes an egg as binder.

For nut roasts and similar recipes, 1 tablespoonful of gram flour (also called besan flour or chick pea flour) beaten with 1 tablespoonful of water makes an effective binder.

A substitute for egg whites made in this country is Edifas A (for the supplier's address, see p.18). This will even make meringues.

For a vegan version of Scrambled Eggs see p.30.

For Eggless Egg Sandwich Spread see p.31.

Mayonnaise

Alfonal *Sun-O-Life* dressing resembles mayonnaise in taste and texture and is completely vegan. *Waistline* salad dressing is also vegan but less nutritious. It is possible to make a home-made mayonnaise with soya flour, tinned soya milk or *Granogen*, but I have never found any of these at all satisfactory.

For Tofu Mayonnaise see p.29.

2.
TOFU – THE WONDER FOOD

The value of the soya bean as a protein source is well known, and some readers may wonder why it appears so infrequently in this book, except in the form of soya milk. The answer is that whereas commercial soya milks are easy to digest, the bean itself, no matter how long it is cooked, causes flatulence in anyone with a delicate digestion. Fortunately there is a way of turning soya beans into an amazingly versatile food which retains all of the protein value yet will be found easily digestible by even the most awkward stomach. That food is tofu, also known as soya bean curd.

Once the bean has been turned into a liquid and the liquid into a curd, the end product can be sliced, mashed, deep fried or *puréed*, and because it is basically bland in flavour it can be used in both sweet and savoury dishes. Tofu can be bought ready-made at some wholefood shops and Chinese speciality shops. (The latter variety tends to have a more distinctive flavour and would not be suitable for sweets.) A packet of do-it-yourself tofu from Japan is also sold in some oriental shops, but it is a variety known as 'silken tofu' which is very soft and not usable for many dishes. A long-life 'silken tofu' is sold pre-packed under the brand name 'Morinaga'. Although it remains fresh for six months if not opened, no chemicals have been added to it; the process is entirely natural. This silken tofu is more versatile as it can be firmed up somewhat by wrapping it in a tea-towel to extract some of the moisture, although it still remains much softer and more liquid than regular tofu. Making tofu at home is not difficult, and the end product works out very inexpensive.

HOME-MADE TOFU

You will need a small wooden or plastic box (a sandwich container is fine) with holes punched in the bottom and sides, and a small square of cheese-cloth to fit in it.

1. Follow the instructions for making home-made soya milk on p. 14.

2. After simmering the milk for a few minutes, dissolve ½ teaspoonful Epsom salts (or nigari if you can get it at a wholefood shop) in a little hot water. Stir this gently into the soya milk. Leave to curdle for about 5 minutes.

3. Place the box with the cheese-cloth in it in a colander in the sink. Carefully pour the contents of the saucepan into the box, so that the liquid flows through and the curd remains. Cover the curd with the top of the cheese-cloth.

4. Place the colander with the box over the saucepan, place a weight on top and leave to stand for about 1 hour.

5. Turn the tofu into a storage container and cover with cold water. Refrigerate. Tofu will keep for several days in the fridge.

Tofu can also be made from soya flour. This is much simpler and less time-consuming, but the resulting product will lack cohesiveness; it can be used in recipes requiring mashed or *puréed* tofu but cannot be sliced or deep fried.

SOYA FLOUR TOFU

1. Whisk 1 part soya flour into 3 parts boiling water, making certain that no lumps remain.

2. Simmer for 20 minutes, stirring occasionally.

3. Add the coagulant and proceed according to the instructions in the previous recipe.

The following recipes use tofu sliced into cubes:

TOFU AND ONIONS

1 lb (½ kilo) tofu
3 onions
3 tablespoonsful vegetable oil
¼ pint (150 ml) water
1 dessertspoonful cornflour
1 dessertspoonful soya sauce
10 oz (300 g) short grain brown rice

1. Cook the rice until tender and keep warm.

2. Slice the onions thinly and *sauté* them in the oil until they become tender.

3. Cut the tofu into small cubes and add it to the onions. Stir well.

4. Combine the cornflour with the water and soya sauce. Pour the mixture over the tofu and onions. Bring to the boil, stirring constantly until thickened.

5. Simmer for 2-3 minutes then serve over the cooked rice.

SWEET AND SOUR TOFU AND VEGETABLES

1 lb (½ kilo) tofu
1 medium-sized tin pineapple chunks
1 lb (½ kilo) tomatoes
1 bunch spring onions
3 oz (75 g) almonds
4 tablespoonsful vegetable oil
4 tablespoonsful soya sauce
1 dessertspoonful cornflour
10 oz (300 g) short grain brown rice

1. Cook the brown rice until tender and keep warm.

2. Cut the tofu into small cubes. Mince the spring onions. *Sauté* them both in the oil for 3 minutes.

3. Chop the tomatoes and add them to the pan. Cook for 5 minutes.

4. Drain the pineapple, rinse, and add to the pan along with the whole almonds. Cook for 2-3 minutes.

5. Dissolve the cornflour in the soya sauce and pour the mixture over the vegetables and tofu. Stir well until thickened and simmer for a minute or two.

6. Serve over the cooked brown rice.

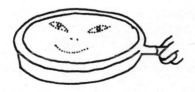

The following recipes use tofu *puréed:*

MUSHROOM STROGANOFF

1 lb (½ kilo) mushrooms
4 tablespoonsful vegetable oil
2 oz (50g) wholemeal flour
¾ pint (400 ml) vegetable stock
1 clove garlic
1 onion
12 oz (350g) tofu
Sea salt, freshly ground black pepper, and mustard powder
  to taste
10 oz (300g) wholemeal noodles

1. Cook the noodles until tender and keep warm.

2. Slice the mushrooms and *sauté* them in the oil until tender.

3. Chop the onion and garlic finely and add them to the saucepan. *Sauté* for a further 5 minutes.

4. Add the flour, stirring well. Slowly add the vegetable stock, stirring constantly to avoid lumps. Cook for a minute or two.

5. Put the tofu in the liquidizer and add enough water to make about 1 pint (½ litre) of tofu cream. Liquidize thoroughly.

6. Add the tofu cream to the mushroom mixture, stirring well. Season and cook until well heated, then serve over the cooked noodles.

TOFU MAYONNAISE

10 oz (300 g) tofu
⅓ pint (200 ml) vegetable oil
4 tablespoonsful lemon juice or cider vinegar
1 dessertspoonful soya sauce

1. Liquidize all of the above ingredients together until thick and creamy. Store in the fridge.

The following recipes use tofu as an egg substitute:

TOFU 'SCRAMBLED EGGS'

1 lb (½ kilo) tofu
2 tablespoonsful vegetable oil
½ teaspoonful onion salt
1 tablespoonful soya sauce
½ teaspoonful turmeric
Smokey Snaps (optional)

1. Mash the tofu and combine with the rest of the ingredients, except the oil.

2. Heat the oil and add the tofu mixture. Stir well over a high heat until well heated.

3. Serve on wholemeal toast if desired.

TOFU PIPÉRADE

4 tablespoonsful olive oil
1 large onion
2 cloves garlic
1 medium-sized green pepper
1 medium-sized red pepper
4 large tomatoes
½ teaspoonful thyme
½ teaspoonful oregano
Sea salt and freshly ground black pepper to taste
12 oz (350g) tofu
½ teaspoonful turmeric

1. Slice the onion thinly, crush the garlic cloves and thinly slice the peppers.

2. *Sauté* the above in the oil until tender but not brown.

3. Peel and chop the tomatoes. Add them to the pan along with the herbs and seasoning.

4. Cook, stirring occasionally, for about 10 more minutes.

5. Mash the tofu with the turmeric and add to the pan. Cook for several minutes more, stirring constantly, until the mixture is well heated.

6. Serve on toast or on brown rice or with potatoes.

EGGLESS EGG SANDWICH SPREAD

½ lb (¼ kilo) tofu
¼ teaspoonful turmeric
1 stalk celery
1 small onion
1 tablespoonful Sun-O-Life dressing (or tofu mayonnaise)
1 tablespoonful minced parsley
1 teaspoonful brewer's yeast (optional)
½ teaspoonful mustard powder
Sea salt (or celery salt) to taste

1. Mash the tofu. Mince the onion and celery.

2. Combine all the ingredients and store in the fridge.

The following recipes use tofu in sweet dishes:

TOFU CHEESECAKE I

1 lb (½ kilo) tofu
3 tablespoonsful soya flour
4 teaspoonsful vanilla extract
Juice and grated rind of 2 lemons
2 heaped teaspoonsful agar-agar
6 oz (200g) raw cane sugar
1 heaped teaspoonful baking powder
4 oz (100g) cornflakes
1 oz (25g) polyunsaturated margarine
1 teaspoonful cinnamon
2 tablespoonsful desiccated coconut

1. Mash the tofu. Add the soya flour, vanilla extract, lemon juice and rind, agar-agar, baking powder and sugar – leaving about 2 tablespoonsful of the sugar aside. Mix very thoroughly.

2. Melt the margarine; crush the cornflakes and mix them with the melted margarine. Turn into a flan tin or pie dish and smooth down to make a pie crust.

3. Pour the tofu mixture into the cornflake pie crust.

4. Mix the remaining sugar with the coconut and cinnamon and sprinkle this over the tofu mixture.

5. Bake in a slow oven 275°F/140°C (Gas Mark 1) for an hour and a half. Cool slightly (or completely) before serving.

TOFU CHEESECAKE II

6 oz (200g) vegan digestive biscuits (e.g. Mitchelhills)
2 oz (50g) polyunsaturated margarine
1 lb (½ kilo) tofu
3 tablespoonsful tahini
4 oz (100g) + 2 tablespoonsful raw cane sugar
2 dessertspoonsful lemon juice
½ teaspoonful sea salt
1½ teaspoonsful pure vanilla essence
½ pint (¼ litre) thick soya yogurt (see p. 20)
¼ teaspoonful cinnamon

1. Melt the margarine; crush the biscuits and mix them with
    the melted margarine. Place the mixture in a pie dish and
    form into a crust.

2. *Purée* the tofu then mix it with the tahini, 4 oz (100g) of the
    sugar, the lemon juice, salt and half of the vanilla essence.

3. Spoon this mixture into the shell and bake in a moderate
    oven at 350°F/180°C (Gas Mark 4) for about half an hour,
    until the filling has set and is golden on top. Allow to cool to
    room temperature.

4. Mix the soya yogurt, 2 tablespoonsful sugar and remaining
    vanilla essence together.

5. Sprinkle the top of the cake with the cinnamon, then pour
    over the yogurt mixture.

6. Bake in a hot oven at 425°F/220°C (Gas Mark 7) for 5
    minutes. Allow to cool, then chill thoroughly until ready to
    serve.

3.
SOUPS, SALADS AND SNACKS

LENTIL AND BARLEY SOUP

4 oz (100g) brown lentils
2 oz (50g) pot barley
1 large onion
2 stalks celery
2 carrots
2 pints (1 litre) water
2 teaspoonsful dried mixed herbs
1 tablespoonful miso paste

1. Cover the lentils and barley with boiling water and leave to soak for a few hours or overnight. Drain well and rinse thoroughly.

2. Chop all the vegetables finely.

3. Mix together the lentils, barley and chopped vegetables and cover them with water. Bring to the boil, adding the herbs.

4. Simmer for 30-40 minutes until the lentils and barley are tender. Remove a little of the liquid and mix together with miso paste until smooth. Return this to the saucepan, mix thoroughly and serve.

COLD CARROT SOUP

½lb (¼ kilo) carrots
1 tablespoonful grated onion
2 tablespoonsful peanut butter
¼ pint (150 ml) water
½ pint (¼ litre) soya milk

1. Clean and slice the carrots; cover them with water and boil gently for 20 minutes.

2. Add the grated onion and peanut butter and simmer for 20 minutes more.

3. Cool slightly and *purée* the soup in a liquidizer.

4. Add the soya milk and mix well.

5. Chill for several hours before serving.

CORN AND CURRY SOUP

2 tins creamed-style sweet corn
¾ pint (400 ml) soya milk
1 tablespoonful grated onion
1 heaped teaspoonful curry powder
1 tablespoonful polyunsaturated margarine
Sprinkling of paprika

1. Combine all the ingredients except the last two in a liquidizer and blend thoroughly.

2. Pour the soup into a saucepan and heat gently. Simmer for 10 minutes.

3. Add the margarine and mix in well.

4. Sprinkle paprika on the top when serving.

MISO SOUP

1 onion
1 large carrot
1 small or ½ large head white cabbage
1 tablespoonful vegetable oil
3 tablespoonsful miso paste
2 pints (1 litre) water

1. Slice the onions thinly, cut the carrot into matchsticks, and shred the cabbage.

2. *Sauté* the onions for 2 minutes, then add the carrot and cabbage and *sauté* them for 5-10 minutes longer, stirring constantly.

3. Add the water, bring to the boil and simmer for 20 minutes.

4. Remove some of the liquid and mix it in a cup with the miso paste until the paste is dissolved. Add this to the soup, mix thoroughly and serve.

POTATO AND CARROT SOUP

1½ lb (¾ kilo) potatoes
1 lb (½ kilo) carrots
1 small onion
3 oz (75 g) polyunsaturated margarine
1 teaspoonful raw cane sugar
2 pints (1 litre) water
Sea salt and freshly ground black pepper to taste
A little grated nutmeg
Chopped parsley

1. Peel the potatoes and cut them into slices. Slice the onion and carrots.

2. Melt half the margarine, add the onion and cook until softened but not brown. Add the potatoes and carrots and stir well.

3. Add the sugar and a little salt, then add the water and cook until the vegetables are tender.

4. Cool slightly, then put into a liquidizer and *purée*.

5. Return the soup to the pan, reheat and season to taste. Stir in the remaining margarine and a little freshly chopped parsley.

SUMMER VEGETABLE SOUP

2 medium-sized onions
3 medium-sized carrots
2 sticks celery
1 tablespoonful polyunsaturated margarine
1 small can tomato *purée*
1 Morga vegetable stock cube
Sea salt and freshly ground black pepper to taste
1 oz (25 g) wholemeal spaghetti
2 oz (50 g) fresh or frozen green beans
4 oz (100 g) cabbage
2 heaped teaspoonsful wholemeal flour
2 pints (1 litre) water

1. Slice the onions, carrots and celery.

2. Melt the margarine and add the vegetables, *sautéeing* gently for 3-4 minutes without browning. Stir in the tomato *purée*, stock cube, water, salt and pepper.

3. Bring to the boil and simmer for 10 minutes.

4. Break the spaghetti into small pieces, add them to the soup and simmer for a further 10 minutes.

5. Shred the cabbage (and the beans if fresh). Add them to the soup and simmer for 5-10 minutes longer until the spaghetti is tender.

6. Mix the flour with a little cold water in a cup. Add this to the soup, stirring well, and cook for another minute before serving.

CURRIED PEA SOUP

1 medium-sized tin peas
1 tablespoonful grated onion
1 heaped teaspoonful curry powder
Sea salt to taste
1 oz (25 g) polyunsaturated margarine
¾ pint (400 ml) water + 6 tablespoonsful Granogen powder
  or 1½ tins plant milk + ¼ pint (150 ml) water

1. Liquidize all the ingredients except the margarine.

2. Pour the mixture into a saucepan and heat gently. Add the margarine and mix in well.

3. Serve when well heated.

CREAM OF PEANUT BUTTER SOUP

2 celery tops
½ pint (¼ litre) water
1 teaspoonful sea salt
1 oz (25 g) polyunsaturated margarine
1 tablespoonful grated onion
4 stalks celery
2 tablespoonsful wholemeal flour
3 tablespoonsful peanut butter
¾ pint (400 ml) soya milk
Freshly ground black pepper to taste
Paprika

1. Chop the celery tops and cook them in the water with the salt for about 10 minutes. Strain, reserving the water but discarding the celery tops.

2. Mince the celery finely. *Sauté* this with the onion in the margarine for 2 minutes.

3. Stir in the flour. When well blended, add the peanut butter and mix well.

4. Stir in the soya milk and celery water. Stir over a low heat until the mixture boils. Simmer for 2-3 minutes.

5. Season to taste with black pepper. When serving, sprinkle with paprika.

CABBAGE AND APPLE SALAD

1 small white cabbage
3 dessert apples
2 stalks celery
2 small raw beetroots
2 carrots
2 tablespoonsful raisins
2 very ripe bananas
Vegetable oil and lemon juice as required

1. Mince the celery, grate the carrot, apple and beetroot and shred the cabbage.

2. Mix the vegetables together with the raisins in a bowl.

3. Mash the bananas. Add the oil and lemon juice, beating well after each addition until the texture resembles that of mayonnaise.

4. Mix well with the salad and serve.

MACARONI AND KIDNEY BEAN SALAD

½ lb (¼ kilo) wholemeal macaroni
6 oz (200g) kidney beans (these should be boiled for at
  least 10 minutes during cooking)
4 stalks celery
½ green pepper
4 spring onions (or more if desired)
1 teaspoonful raw cane sugar
Sea salt and freshly ground black pepper to taste
5 tablespoonsful vegetable oil
3 tablespoonsful cider vinegar
3 oz (75g) walnuts
2 (or more) tablespoonsful Smokey Snaps
Crisp lettuce leaves

1. Cook the macaroni, rinse in cold water and drain.

2. Combine this with the well-cooked and cooled beans.

3. Chop the celery, green pepper and spring onions finely.
   Chop the walnuts coarsely.

4. Add the vegetables and nuts to the macaroni and bean
   mixture.

5. Combine the oil, vinegar, sugar and seasoning. Add this to
   the salad and mix well.

6. Turn the mixture into a lettuce-lined bowl, sprinkle with
   Smokey Snaps and serve.

ITALIAN BREAD SALAD

1 lb (½ kilo) stale wholemeal bread
¼ pint (150 ml) water
1 clove garlic
1 medium-sized onion
6 oz (200g) tomatoes
3 tablespoonsful vegetable oil
1 tablespoonful cider vinegar
2 teaspoonsful dried basil
Sea salt and freshly ground black pepper to taste

1. Dice the bread, soak it in the water for 10 minutes or more. Drain out the surplus moisture.

2. Crush the garlic and rub the salad bowl with it.

3. Chop the onion finely and peel and dice the tomatoes.

4. Combine the bread with the onion and tomatoes. Add the oil and vinegar with the seasoning and mix lightly together.

5. Sprinkle with basil and serve.

CARIBBEAN SALAD

1 medium-sized tin pineapple chunks
½ green pepper
½ red pepper
4 stalks celery
4 tablespoonsful coarsely chopped walnuts
4-6 tablespoonsful Sun-O-Life dressing
Lemon juice to taste

1. Chop the peppers and celery and drain the pineapple.

2. Combine all the ingredients and serve.

CHICK PEA AND WALNUT SALAD

6 oz (200g) chick peas
4 oz (100g) walnuts
6 tablespoonsful lemon juice
4 tablespoonsful vegetable oil
2 cloves crushed garlic
1 teaspoonful sea salt
Hearts of 2 heads Cos lettuce

1. Cook the soaked chick peas until tender; drain, rinse and leave them to cool.

2. Mash the beans until they are the consistency of coarse crumbs.

3. Chop the walnuts finely and combine them with the mashed beans.

4. Combine the lemon juice, oil, garlic and salt and mix this dressing with the walnuts and beans.

5. Serve at room temperature, spooned into the centre of a shallow dish. Surround with small Cos lettuce leaves to use as scoopers.

FRUIT AND NUT COLE SLAW

1 small white cabbage
2 dessert apples
1 small tin pineapple chunks
4 oz (100g) salted peanuts
4 fl oz (100ml) Sun-O-Life dressing

1. Shred the cabbage and dice the apple.

2. Combine all the ingredients in a salad bowl and serve.

BEAN AND ALMOND SALAD

1 lb (½ kilo) runner beans (or frozen green beans)
2 oz (50g) almonds
4 tomatoes
1 small onion
1 oz (25g) polyunsaturated margarine
2 oz (50g) sultanas or raisins
2 tablespoonsful vegetable oil
2 tablespoonsful cider vinegar
Pinch of raw cane sugar
Sea salt and freshly ground black pepper to taste

1. Wash, string and slice the beans and cook them until tender. Drain them well and leave to cool.

2. Shred the almonds finely. Peel and chop the tomatoes and onions.

3. Melt the margarine in a saucepan, add the onion, almonds and sultanas and *sauté* them until the onion is tender.

4. Combine the oil, vinegar and seasoning.

5. Mix together the beans, onion mixture, tomatoes and dressing in a bowl.

6. Chill and serve.

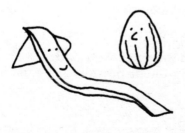

BRUSSELS SPROUTS SALAD

1 lb (½ kilo) Brussels sprouts
4 carrots
2 tablespoonsful lemon juice
4 tablespoonsful Sun-O-Life dressing
4 tablespoonsful chopped dates
1 bunch watercress

1.　Coarsely grate the sprouts and finely grate the carrots.

2.　Mix these together with the lemon juice, dates and dressing.

3.　Serve on a bed of watercress.

POTATO AND ARTICHOKE HEART SALAD

1 lb (½ kilo) potatoes
1 medium-sized tin artichoke hearts
4 tablespoonsful olive oil
Sea salt and freshly ground black pepper to taste
1 dessertspoonful lemon juice
2 oz (50g) walnuts
Crisp lettuce leaves as required

1.　Cook the potatoes until tender. (They can then be peeled if desired, but this is not necessary.) Quarter them and sprinkle with 1 tablespoonful olive oil while still warm.

2.　Chop the walnuts and combine them with the potatoes.

3.　Drain the tinned artichoke hearts and arrange them on lettuce leaves with the potatoes and walnuts.

4.　Combine the remaining olive oil with the lemon juice and seasoning and pour over the salad.

SALAD NIÇOISE

1 lb (½ kilo) fresh or frozen French beans
6 large tomatoes
2 large potatoes
4 tablespoonsful olive oil
2 tablespoonsful cider vinegar
¼ teaspoonful mustard powder
Sea salt and freshly ground black pepper to taste
1 tablespoonful capers
2 oz (50g) olives

1. Cook the beans and potatoes (separately) until tender. Leave to cool and slice them.

2. Quarter the tomatoes and arrange them with the beans and potatoes on individual salad plates.

3. Combine the olive oil, cider vinegar, mustard and seasoning and pour this over the salad.

4. Mince the olives, combine them with the capers and sprinkle over the salad.

GREEN BEAN AND PIMENTO SALAD

1 small tin pimentos
1lb (½ kilo) fresh or frozen sliced green beans
2 medium-sized carrots
4 tablespoonsful Sun-O-Life dressing

1. Drain the pimentos and slice them into thin strips.

2. Cook the beans until just tender, drain and leave to cool.

3. Grate the carrots coarsely.

4. Combine all the ingredients and serve.

CURRIED BUTTER BEAN SALAD

6oz (200g) butter beans (these should be boiled for at least
  10 minutes during cooking)
¼pint (150ml) Sun-O-Life dressing
1 heaped tablespoonful mango chutney
1 heaped tablespoonful desiccated coconut
2 heaped teaspoonsful curry powder

1. Cook the butter beans (which have been soaked overnight) until tender.

2. Combine the dressing, chutney, curry powder and coconut. Add the butter beans, mix and serve.

STUFFED PEAR SALAD

4 ripe pears
6 oz (200 g) dates
3 oz (75 g) walnuts
3 tablespoonsful vegetable oil
1½ tablespoonsful lemon juice
Crisp lettuce leaves as required

1. Chop the dates and walnuts. Peel and halve the pears, remove the cores and some of the flesh to leave a hollow for the filling. (The flesh can be chopped into the filling.)

2. Combine the dates, walnuts, oil and lemon juice with the chopped flesh and pile the mixture into the pear halves.

3. Serve on crisp lettuce leaves.

STUFFED BANANA SALAD

4 small bananas
2 oz (50 g) peanut butter
1 oz (25 g) raisins or sultanas
2 tablespoonsful Sun-O-Life dressing
2 tablespoonsful salted peanuts
Crisp lettuce leaves as required

1. Chop the raisins finely. Mix them together with the peanut butter.

2. Peel and split the bananas lengthwise and fill them sandwich fashion with the peanut butter-raisin mixture.

3. Spoon the dressing over the bananas and top with the salted peanuts.

4. Serve on crisp lettuce leaves

MEXICAN-STYLE POTATO SALAD

1 lb (½ kilo) new potatoes
1 tablespoonful vegetable oil
1 tablespoonful cider vinegar
1 large tin sweet corn with red and green peppers
2 tablespoonsful Smokey Snaps
¼ pint (150 ml) soya yogurt (see p. 20)
1 bunch watercress
Sea salt and freshly ground black pepper to taste

1. Cook the potatoes until tender, drain and dice them.

2. Combine the oil and vinegar, pour this over diced potatoes and leave until cold.

3. Drain the sweet corn and mix it with the yogurt and seasoning. Combine this with the potatoes.

4. Pile onto a serving dish and surround with sprigs of watercress. Sprinkle Smokey Snaps over the salad just before serving.

TOMATO AND ONION SAVOURY

8 slices wholemeal toast spread with polyunsaturated margarine
2 oz (50g) polyunsaturated margarine
2 large onions
1 dozen medium-sized or large very ripe tomatoes
Pinch of oregano
2 teaspoonsful raw cane sugar
Sea salt and freshly ground black pepper to taste

1. Slice the onions and chop the tomatoes coarsely.

2. Heat the margarine and *sauté* the sliced onions until golden.

Add the tomatoes and seasonings.

3. Simmer gently for approximately 15 minutes until the tomatoes are tender.

4. Serve immediately on hot 'buttered' toast.

CURRY SPREAD

1 medium-sized onion
2 cloves garlic
2 bay leaves
12 whole cloves
2 oz (50g) polyunsaturated margarine
1 tablespoonful curry powder
½ pint (¼ litre) tomato ketchup
1 teaspoonful cider vinegar

1. Slice the onions and chop the garlic finely.

2. Heat the margarine and *sauté* the onion and garlic until brown.

3. Stir in the curry powder and add the tomato ketchup, vinegar, cloves and bay leaves. Simmer for 20 minutes until thick then remove cloves and bay leaves.

4. Serve hot on wholemeal toast or chilled on crispbread or crackers.

MUSHROOM SPREAD

1 lb (½ kilo) mushrooms
2 medium-sized onions
1 tablespoonful vegetable oil
1 tablespoonful polyunsaturated margarine
1-2 tablespoonsful soya yogurt (see p. 20)
Sea salt and freshly ground black pepper to taste

1. Chop the mushrooms and onions.

2. *Sauté* them in the oil and margarine until tender.

3. Finely chop, mash or liquidize the mixture.

4. Add the soya yogurt and seasoning to taste.

5. Serve chilled on wholemeal bread or toast.

GRILLED GARLIC MUSHROOMS

1 lb (½ kilo) mushrooms
4 oz (100g) polyunsaturated margarine
2 cloves garlic
8 small slices wholemeal toast

1. Clean the mushrooms and remove the stems.

2. Crush the garlic and *sauté* it in the margarine over a very low flame.

3. Fill the mushroom caps with the garlic-margarine mixture. Place in a shallow baking pan and grill for 5-7 minutes.

4. Soak up the margarine which has run out of the caps with the toast; place the mushrooms on the toast and serve hot.

SOYA BEAN SPREAD

1 large onion
2 cloves garlic
2 oz (50g) parsley
6 oz (200g) soya beans (these should be boiled for at least
  10 minutes during cooking)
1 oz (25g) Smokey Snaps
1 teaspoonful oregano
1 tablespoonful soya sauce
¼ pint (150 ml) Sun-O-Life dressing
1 tablespoonful vegetable oil

1. Chop the onion finely and crush the garlic.

2. *Sauté* the onion and garlic in oil until tender.

3. Mash the cooked soya beans.

4. Add the *sautéed* onions and garlic and all remaining ingredients. Mix together well and serve chilled.

4.
CEREALS AND PASTA

Brown rice, whole wheat grains and pot barley should be covered with boiling water and soaked for several hours, then drained and washed. Then cover them with cold water, add salt, bring to the boil and simmer for 20-25 minutes until the water is absorbed.

Millet and bulgur wheat require no pre-soaking but should be washed. They can be *sautéed* in vegetable oil before being covered with water if desired. Approximately three times the amount of grain used is the correct ratio of water for cooking these grains. They should only require 15-20 minutes cooking time.

Wholemeal pasta takes longer to cook than ordinary pasta. Proprietary brand packets often give cooking instructions. Be sure to check ingredients as some pastas are made with eggs. If buying pasta loose, the following is a rough guide to cooking times:

Spaghetti	10-15 minutes
Macaroni	10 minutes
Lasagne	20 minutes
Noodles	15 minutes

Pasta should always be cooked *al dente* – i.e. 'have a bit of a bite', but fortunately it is much harder to overcook wholemeal pasta.

CREOLE-STYLE NOODLES

12 oz (350g) wholemeal noodles
2 onions
2 oz (50g) polyunsaturated margarine
2 green peppers
2 lb (1 kilo) tomatoes
½ lb (¼ kilo) French or runner beans
4 oz (100g) fresh okra
Sea salt to taste

1. Cook the noodles for 10 minutes in boiling salted water, then leave them to drain.

2. Chop the onions and *sauté* them in the margarine until beginning to soften.

3. Peel and chop the tomatoes and chop the green pepper and green beans. Remove both ends of the okra, cut them into small pieces and cover with boiling water for 1 minute, then drain.

4. Add all of the vegetables to the onions, cover and simmer for 20 minutes.

5. Add the noodles and cook until they are tender, adding water if necessary. Season to taste and serve.

ORIENTAL MACARONI

12 oz (350g) wholemeal macaroni
2 tablespoonsful vegetable oil
1 bunch spring onions
4 stalks celery
4 oz (100g) fresh or frozen French or runner beans
4 oz (100g) fresh bean sprouts
½ pint (¼ litre) water
2 tablespoonsful brown rice flour
1 tablespoonful soya flour
½ small tin water chestnuts
2 tablespoonsful soya sauce
½ teaspoonful garlic salt
½ small tin pimentos
1 tablespoonful sunflower seeds
½ Morga vegetable stock cube

1. Cook the macaroni until tender, drain and keep warm.

2. Mince the spring onions and celery and *sauté* them in the oil for 2-3 minutes.

3. Slice the beans and add them to the saucepan along with most of the water (retaining about ¼ cupful) and the half broth cube. Bring to the boil, cover and simmer for 5 minutes.

4. Mix the rice flour and soya flour with the remaining water. Add this to the saucepan, stirring until thickened.

5. Slice the water chestnuts and dice the tinned pimento.

6. Add all the remaining ingredients and mix thoroughly. Stir until everything is heated through, then pour over the macaroni and mix well.

RICE AND VEGETABLE SAVOURY

10 oz (300 g) long grain brown rice
½ pint (¼ litre) tomato juice
Water as required
2 large aubergines
1 lb (½ kilo) fresh or frozen shelled peas
4 large carrots
4-6 tablespoonsful vegetable oil

1. Soak the rice overnight. Drain, place in a saucepan and add the tomato juice, 1 tablespoonful of oil and enough water to cover. Bring to the boil, lower the heat and simmer until the liquid is absorbed and the rice is tender.

2. Dice the carrots and cook them with the peas in boiling salted water until just tender. Set aside to drain.

3. Dice the aubergines and fry them in the rest of the vegetable oil until tender.

4. Place half the rice in a greased baking dish. Cover this with the vegetables and top with another layer of rice. Press down slightly.

5. Bake in a moderate oven at 350°F/180°C (Gas Mark 4) for 15-20 minutes.

MILLET CASSEROLE

½ lb (¼ kilo) millet
Sea salt to taste
2 onions
1½ pints (¾ litre) boiling water
2 carrots
1 small or ½ medium-sized cabbage
3 fl oz (80 ml) vegetable oil
1 oz (25 g) wholemeal flour
½ pint (¼ litre) water
1-2 tablespoonsful soya sauce
1 oz (25 g) wholemeal breadcrumbs

1. Chop the onion, cut the carrots into slivers and shred the cabbage.

2. *Sauté* the millet in 2 tablespoonsful of the oil until it is beginning to brown. Cover with the boiling water and salt. Simmer for about 20 minutes.

3. *Sauté* the vegetables in 2 tablespoonsful of the oil until tender.

4. In a separate saucepan, heat the remaining oil, add the flour and stir well. Slowly add the water, stirring constantly to avoid lumps. Add the soya sauce and bring to the boil. Simmer for 2-3 minutes.

5. In a greased baking dish, place alternate layers of millet, vegetables and sauce, ending with a layer of sauce. Sprinkle with the breadcrumbs.

6. Bake in a moderate oven at 350°F/180°C (Gas Mark 4) for about 20 minutes until the top is lightly browned.

CREAMY CURRIED SAUCE ON BULGUR

½lb (¼ kilo) bulgur wheat
3 tablespoonsful vegetable oil
1 teaspoonful (or more to taste) curry powder
Sea salt to taste
4 small leeks
4 stalks celery
½lb (¼ kilo) mushrooms
½ pint (¼ litre) soya yogurt (see p. 20)

1. Cook the bulgur wheat in salted water until tender.

2. Heat the oil and add the curry powder. Cook over a gentle heat for 1 minute.

3. Slice the leeks finely and chop the celery and mushrooms, then stir-fry them in the seasoned oil for a few minutes, until just tender.

4. Turn off the heat, stir in the yogurt and mix well.

5. Serve the sauce over the cooked bulgur wheat.

STIR-FRIED VEGETABLES WITH BARLEY

½ lb (¼ kilo) pot barley
Sea salt to taste
3 small leeks
2 carrots
4 stalks celery
½ lb (¼ kilo) mushrooms
4 tablespoonsful vegetable oil
1 teaspoonful (or more to taste) ground cumin seed
2 tablespoonsful sunflower seeds

1. Cook the barley in salted water until tender.

2. Slice the leeks thinly, cut the carrots into matchsticks, chop the celery and mushrooms.

3. Heat the oil gently, add the cumin and stir well.

4. Add the vegetables to the oil and stir-fry for a few minutes until the vegetables are just tender.

5. Toast the sunflower seeds under the grill until slightly roasted.

6. Combine the cooked barley, vegetables and sunflower seeds, stirring well, and serve.

BANANA AND SPAGHETTI CURRY

10 oz (300g) wholemeal spaghetti
3 large bananas
2 oz (50g) polyunsaturated margarine
2 oz (50g) sultanas or raisins
½ pint (¼ litre) soya milk
1 small onion
1½ oz (40g) wholemeal flour
2 teaspoonsful (or more to taste) curry powder
2 teaspoonsful chutney
¼ pint (150ml) water from spaghetti

1. Cook the spaghetti in boiling salted water until tender, then drain, reserving ¼ pint (150ml) of the water.

2. Chop the onion finely, melt the margarine and *sauté* the onion gently for 5 minutes.

3. Stir in the flour and curry powder, then add the soya milk and spaghetti water, stirring constantly to avoid lumps.

4. Bring to the boil, then add the raisins and chutney.

5. Cut the bananas into ½ inch slices and add them to the sauce. Simmer gently for 10 minutes.

6. Place the spaghetti in a heated serving dish and pour the sauce over.

TOMATO AND RICE LOAF

½ lb (¼ kilo) short grain brown rice
½ lb (¼ kilo) tomatoes
2 stalks celery
3 oz (75 g) wholemeal breadcrumbs
⅓ pint (200 ml) soya milk
1 tablespoonful vegetable oil
½ teaspoonful garlic salt
½ teaspoonful onion salt

1. Cook the rice until tender.

2. Chop the tomatoes and celery and *sauté* them in the oil until tender.

3. Combine all of the ingredients, including the rice, and mix well.

4. Pour the mixture into an oiled loaf tin and bake in a moderate oven at 350°F/180°C (Gas Mark 4) for 30 minutes.

MIXED VEGETABLES WITH PASTA

4 tablespoonsful olive oil
1 bunch fresh parsley (about 8 tablespoonsful, chopped)
6 spring onions
2 cloves garlic
1 medium-sized onion
1 tablespoonful basil
½ small head cabbage
½ lb (¼ kilo) courgettes
½ lb (¼ kilo) tomatoes
2 green peppers
½ pint (¼ litre) water
½ Morga vegetable stock cube
2 teaspoonsful cider vinegar
Sea salt and freshly ground black pepper to taste
12-14 oz (350-400g) wholemeal noodles or spaghetti
1 oz (25g) polyunsaturated margarine
4 tablespoonsful Smokey Snaps

1. Chop the parsley, spring onions, garlic and onion finely. *Sauté* them in the oil for 3 minutes.

2. Shred the cabbage, dice the courgettes and green peppers, peel and slice the tomatoes and add these ingredients to the saucepan along with the water, ½ stock cube, cider vinegar, basil and seasoning.

3. Simmer, uncovered, for 10 minutes.

4. Cook the pasta until just tender, then drain and toss with the margarine.

5. Add the vegetable mixture, mix well, and sprinkle with the Smokey Snaps.

BAKED NOODLES AND AUBERGINES

1½ lb (¾ kilo) aubergines
Sea salt as required
14 oz (400 g) wholemeal noodles
1 large onion
1 clove garlic
3 tablespoonsful vegetable oil (or more if required)
2 large tomatoes
2 tablespoonsful tomato *purée*
½ teaspoonful cinnamon
¼ teaspoonful grated nutmeg
¼ teaspoonful (or more to taste) cayenne pepper

1. Slice the aubergines, sprinkle with salt, and leave them in a colander for at least half an hour to allow the bitter juice to drain away. Rinse well and pat dry.

2. Cook the noodles in boiling salted water until just tender. Drain and keep warm.

3. Chop the onion, mince the garlic and *sauté* them in the oil until golden.

4. Add the aubergine slices and fry until lightly browned on both sides, using a little more oil if necessary.

5. Skin and chop the tomatoes and add them to the aubergine mixture along with the tomato *purée*. Season with the spices and add just a little water, simmering gently until the aubergines are tender and you have a thick sauce.

6. Place alternate layers of pasta and sauce in a greased casserole.

7. Bake in a moderate oven at 350°F/180°C (Gas Mark 4) for about 30 minutes.

CREAMY BANANA RISOTTO

½lb (¼ kilo) long grain brown rice
2oz (50g) polyunsaturated margarine
1 small onion
1 green pepper
1oz (25g) wholemeal flour
1 pint (½ litre) soya milk
1 oz (25g) soya flour cheese (see p. 21)
1lb (½ kilo) green-tipped bananas

1. Cook the rice until tender.

2. Chop the onion, slice the green pepper into thin strips and *sauté* them in 1oz (25g) of margarine until tender.

3. Stir this mixture into the cooked rice.

4. Melt the rest of the margarine and stir in the flour. Slowly add the soya milk, stirring constantly to avoid lumps. Bring to the boil and simmer for 1 minute. Add the soya flour cheese and stir until melted.

5. Peel and slice the bananas thinly and mix in with the rice mixture. Season to taste.

6. Put a layer of the rice mixture into a greased baking dish. Cover with a layer of sauce. Repeat the layers until all the ingredients are used up, ending with the sauce.

7. Bake in a moderate oven at 350°F/180°C (Gas Mark 4) for about 30 minutes.

MACARONI AND MUSHROOM LOAF

½ lb (¼ kilo) wholemeal macaroni
2 oz (50g) polyunsaturated margarine
1 onion
2 large tomatoes
6 oz (200g) mushrooms
2 tablespoonsful gram flour (see p.23)
4 tablespoonsful water
Sea salt and freshly ground black pepper to taste
Wholemeal breadcrumbs as required.

1. Cook the macaroni until tender and leave to drain.

2. Chop the onions finely, peel and slice the tomatoes and chop the mushrooms.

3. Heat the margarine and *sauté* the vegetables until tender.

4. Combine the macaroni and vegetables.

5. Add the water to the gram flour and mix well. Add this to the macaroni mixture and mix well.

6. Add enough breadcrumbs to make a sticky consistency and season to taste.

7. Put into a greased loaf tin and bake in a moderate oven at 350°F/180°C (Gas Mark 4) for 30-40 minutes.

5.
PULSE DISHES

The standard procedure for all pulses except split red lentils is as follows: Pour boiling water over the beans in a saucepan and bring to the boil for a minute or two. Cover the beans and leave them to soak for several hours or overnight. Drain the beans and rinse them (do *not* use the soaking water to cook them in). Cover them again with cold water, bring to boiling point for ten minutes and then simmer until cooked. Add salt only towards the end of the cooking time (salt retards the softening process).

Approximate cooking times for pulses in this chapter:

Butter beans	1½ hours
Haricot beans	1 hour
Chick peas	1½ hours
Split peas	30 minutes
Aduki beans	45 minutes
Black-eyed beans	45 minutes
Red kidney beans	1 hour
Brown lentils	30 minutes
Red lentils (unsoaked)	20 minutes

BEAN CASSEROLE

¾ lb (350g) butter or haricot beans
1½ lb (¾ kilo) mixed root vegetables (carrots, turnips, swedes)
½ lb (¼ kilo) potatoes
1 small head celery
3 medium-sized onions
2 oz (50g) polyunsaturated margarine
2 rounded teaspoonsful yeast extract
1 medium-sized can tomatoes
2 oz (50g) fresh wholemeal breadcrumbs
½ pint (¼ litre) water

1. Soak the beans overnight; cook until tender then leave to drain.

2. Dice the root vegetables and potatoes (peeled if desired). Trim and slice the celery and the onions.

3. Melt the margarine in a large saucepan. Add the diced vegetables, celery and onion. Stir over a moderate heat for 5 minutes.

4. Stir in the beans, water, yeast extract and the can of tomatoes. Bring to the boil, then transfer to a large casserole.

5. Cover and bake in the centre of a moderate oven at 350°F/180°C (Gas Mark 4) for 1¼-1½ hours until the vegetables are cooked.

6. Remove the lid from the casserole. Sprinkle the breadcrumbs over the vegetables and cook for a further 20-30 minutes in the oven until the topping is crisp and golden.

CHICK PEAS IN SPANISH SAUCE

¾ lb (350g) chick peas
1 green pepper
1 red pepper
1 small chilli pepper
1 onion
1 clove garlic
2 tablespoonsful olive oil
1 tablespoonful chopped parsley
1 teaspoonful sea salt
1 lb (½ kilo) ripe tomatoes

1. Soak the chick peas overnight and cook until tender.

2. Chop the peppers, onions, garlic and tomatoes.

3. Lightly fry the peppers, onion and garlic in the olive oil for a few minutes.

4. Add the parsley, tomatoes and salt and cook on a low heat for about half an hour, stirring occasionally, until the tomatoes are pulped.

5. Combine this mixture with the cooked chick peas and serve it with potatoes or over rice or another grain.

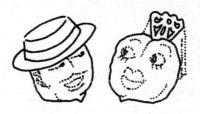

LENTIL CURRY

½ lb (¼ kilo) red lentils
1 teaspoonful sea salt
Freshly ground black pepper
1 bay leaf
2 onions
1 clove garlic
2 tablespoonsful vegetable oil
1 dessert apple
1 tablespoonful curry powder
1 teaspoonful lemon juice
1 small can baked beans (Heinz or other vegan brand)
4-inch piece cucumber
10-12 oz (300-350g) long grain brown rice, cooked

1. Cover the lentils with water, add the salt and bay leaf and simmer until tender (about 20 minutes).

2. Finely chop the onions and garlic. Peel, core and chop the apple and chop the cucumber finely.

3. Heat the oil gently; add the onions, garlic and apple and fry gently until soft and lightly brown. Stir in the curry powder and fry for 2 minutes.

4. Add the lemon juice, baked beans, lentils and chopped cucumber and heat thoroughly. (If desired, add more sea salt and/or freshly ground black pepper at this stage.)

5. Serve over the rice.

ADUKI-VEGETABLE PIE

½ lb (¼ kilo) wholemeal pastry (see p. 11)
1 onion
2 leeks
2 carrots
2 small swedes
1 cooking apple
½ lb (¼ kilo) aduki beans
3 oz (75g) currants
3 oz (75g) walnuts
2 tablespoonsful vegetable oil
Sea salt to taste
Pinch of cinnamon

1. Cover the aduki beans with boiling water and leave to soak for several hours or overnight. Drain, cover with fresh water and cook until tender.

2. Chop the onion, leeks, carrots, swedes and apple. Chop the walnuts separately.

3. *Sauté* the vegetables in the oil until tender.

4. Combine the cooked aduki beans, *sautéed* vegetables, currants, chopped walnuts, salt and cinnamon.

5. Line a pie dish with the pastry (all of it or, if preferred, save some to make strips across the top). Fill with the bean and vegetable mixture.

6. Bake in a moderately hot oven at 375°F/190°C (Gas Mark 5) for about 30 minutes, until the pastry is golden brown.

AUBERGINE AND CHICK PEA 'RAGOUT'

1 large aubergine
2 large onions
4 fl oz (100 ml) olive oil
6 oz (200 g) chick peas
2 medium-sized cans tomatoes
1 teaspoonful dried mint
Sea salt and freshly ground black pepper to taste

1. Soak the chick peas overnight; drain them, cover with fresh water and cook until tender.

2. Chop the aubergine into cubes and chop the onions coarsely. Heat the olive oil gently and *sauté* until tenderized. Add the cooked chick peas, tinned tomatoes, mint and seasoning.

3. Cook uncovered, over a low heat for half an hour.

4. Cool and serve at room temperature.

VIRGINIAN BLACK-EYED BEANS

¾ lb (350 g) black-eyed beans
1 medium-sized onion
1 bay leaf
½ teaspoonful thyme
3 whole cloves
Sea salt and freshly ground black pepper to taste

1. Cover the beans with boiling water, leave to soak for several hours or overnight, then drain.

2. Chop the onion coarsely and combine it with the beans in a saucepan. Cover with water and add the bay leaf, thyme and cloves.

3. Cook over a low heat until the beans are tender (about 45 minutes). If necessary, add additional water to prevent drying out. Season to taste.

4. Serve with Southern Corn Bread (see below).

SOUTHERN CORN BREAD

4 oz (100g) wholemeal flour
4 oz (100g) maize meal
2 tablespoonsful raw cane sugar
4 teaspoonsful baking powder
1 teaspoonful sea salt
⅓ pint (200ml) soya milk
3 oz (75g) polyunsaturated margarine

1. Mix the flour, maize meal, sugar, baking powder and salt in a bowl.

2. Melt the margarine and add it with the soya milk to the dry mixture. Stir just until this is moistened, then immediately pour the batter into a greased baking pan.

3. Bake in a hot oven at 425°F/220°C (Gas Mark 7) for about an hour, until the top is golden and firm and drawing away from the edges of the pan.

QUICK AND EASY CHILLI

½ lb (¼ kilo) red kidney beans
½ lb (¼ kilo) bulgur wheat
4 tablespoonsful vegetable oil
1 large onion
2 medium-sized cans tomatoes
Sea salt to taste
1 teaspoonful (or more to taste) chilli seasoning (*Note: not* Indian chilli powder, but the mixture of Mexican chilli spices by McCormicks and others, available at many supermarkets)

1. Cover the kidney beans with boiling water and soak them for several hours or overnight. Cook until tender in fresh water then leave to drain.

2. Chop the onion and *sauté* it in the oil until beginning to soften.

3. Add the bulgur and cook for 2-3 minutes more, stirring constantly.

4. Add the cans of tomatoes and some more water if needed (the liquid should be about three times the volume of the bulgur wheat). Add the seasoning and the cooked beans.

5. Simmer until tender (about 15 minutes).

CHICK PEA STROGANOFF

1 oz (25 g) polyunsaturated margarine
1 onion
½ lb (¼ kilo) mushrooms
½ lb (¼ kilo) chick peas
4 tablespoonsful vegetable stock or water
¼ teaspoonful freshly grated nutmeg
1 teaspoonful soya sauce
¼ teaspoonful mustard powder
1 dessertspoonful cider vinegar
⅓ pint (200 ml) soya yogurt (see p. 20)
10 oz (300 g) wholemeal noodles

1. Cover the chick peas with boiling water and soak for several hours or overnight. Drain and cook in fresh water until tender.

2. Chop the onion and mushrooms. Melt the margarine and *sauté* the vegetables until soft.

3. Add the stock, seasonings, chick peas and vinegar. Cover and simmer on a low heat for about 10 minutes.

4. Meanwhile, cook the noodles for 10-15 minutes until soft.

5. Add the yogurt to the chick pea mixture over the lowest possible heat, stirring constantly without bringing to the boil, until heated through.

6. Serve over the cooked noodles.

SPAGHETTI AND BUTTER BEAN CASSEROLE

½ lb (¼ kilo) wholemeal spaghetti
4 oz (100g) butter beans
1 large onion
2 cloves garlic
1 small or ½ large red pepper
4 tablespoonsful olive oil
1 medium-sized can tomatoes
1 small can tomato *purée*
1 teaspoonful raw cane sugar
½ teaspoonful oregano
½ teaspoonful thyme
2 tablespoonsful chopped parsley
2 oz (50g) fine wholemeal breadcrumbs
1 oz (25g) polyunsaturated margarine

1. Cover the butter beans with boiling water and soak for several hours or overnight. Drain, and cook in fresh water until tender.

2. Cook the spaghetti in boiling salted water until just tender.

3. Chop the onion, garlic and red pepper finely and *sauté* them in the olive oil until soft but not brown.

4. Liquidize the tomatoes and add them to the saucepan along with the tomato *purée*, sugar and herbs. Mix well and simmer over a low heat for about 20 minutes.

5. Layer the spaghetti, cooked butter beans and tomato sauce in a greased casserole.

6. Melt the margarine and stir in the breadcrumbs.

7. Top the casserole with the breadcrumbs and bake for 45 minutes in a moderate oven at 350°F/180°C (Gas Mark 4).

ARMENIAN BLACK-EYED BEANS AND NUTS

½ lb (¼ kilo) black-eyed beans
2 onions
4 fl oz (100 ml) olive oil
1 teaspoonful raw cane sugar
1 teaspoonful sea salt
1 small can tomatoes
2 teaspoonsful tomato *purée*
5 oz (150g) mixed nuts
2 tablespoonsful chopped parsley

1. Cover the black-eyed beans with boiling water and leave to soak for several hours or overnight. Cook until tender and drain.

2. Chop the onions and *sauté* them in the olive oil until soft. Chop the nuts coarsely.

3. Liquidize the tinned tomatoes and add them to the saucepan with the rest of the ingredients.

4. Simmer for 10 to 15 minutes before serving.

MACARONI AND BEAN 'HOT-POT'

½lb (¼ kilo) wholemeal macaroni
4 tablespoonsful vegetable oil
1 onion
1 green pepper
6oz (200g) mushrooms
2 large tomatoes
1 teaspoonful dried mixed herbs
1 teaspoonful lemon juice
1 medium-sized can curried baked beans

1. Cook the macaroni in salted water until tender.

2. Chop the onion and pepper finely and slice the mushrooms.
    Peel and chop the tomatoes and *sauté* all the vegetables in
    the oil for about 10 minutes.

3. Add the herbs and lemon juice. Then add the beans, mix
    well and heat thoroughly.

4. Add the cooked macaroni, mix well and serve.

ITALIAN LENTILS AND SPAGHETTI

2 onions
2 cloves garlic
1 large carrot
1 green pepper
1 medium-sized can tomatoes
12 oz (350g) red lentils
2 bay leaves
2 teaspoonsful thyme
1 tablespoonful oregano
1 tablespoonful basil
12 oz (350g) wholemeal spaghetti
2 tablespoonsful Smokey Snaps
2 tablespoonsful olive oil

1. Chop the onion, carrots and green pepper coarsely and the garlic very finely. *Sauté* them in the olive oil until tender.

2. Add the tinned tomatoes and the herbs and then the lentils. Add enough water to cover and simmer for 15-20 minutes.

3. Add the pasta and enough additional water to just cover. Cook all the ingredients together until the spaghetti is cooked *al dente* (approximately 10 minutes).

4. Sprinkle with the Smokey Snaps and serve.

LENTIL AND RICE LOAF

6 oz (200g) red lentils
½ lb (¼ kilo) short grain brown rice
1 small onion
1 tablespoonful vegetable oil
1 tablespoonful wholemeal flour
3 tablespoonsful soya milk
½ teaspoonful sage
2 oz (50g) walnuts
Sea salt to taste

1. Cover the rice with boiling water and leave to soak for several hours or overnight. Drain and wash the rice, then cover with salted water and cook until very tender.

2. Cover the lentils with salted water and cook until very tender. Mash well.

3. Chop the onion finely and *sauté* it in the oil until tender. Add the flour and stir well. Then pour in the milk, stirring constantly.

4. Chop the walnuts and add these to the saucepan along with the cooked rice, cooked lentils and the sage. Mix together well.

5. Pack into an oiled bread tin, and bake in a moderate oven at 350°F/180°C (Gas Mark 4) for 30-40 minutes until slightly browned on top.

6.

VEGETABLE-BASED SAVOURIES

POTATO YAHNI

2½lb (1¼ kilos) potatoes
1lb (½ kilo) onions
1lb (½ kilo) tomatoes
1 tablespoonful raw cane sugar
¼ pint (150ml) olive oil
1 bay leaf
Sea salt and freshly ground black pepper to taste

1. Peel the potatoes thinly and cut into uniform size. Chop the onions finely and peel and chop the tomatoes.

2. Heat the oil and fry the onions until golden brown.

3. Add the tomatoes and simmer with the sugar and bay leaf until soft.

4. Add the potatoes, seasoning, and enough water to half cover them.

5. Cook until the potatoes are soft and the sauce is thick. Serve immediately.

MUSHROOM AND TOMATO PIE

1 lb (½ kilo) mushrooms
3 onions
1 stalk celery (optional)
6 tomatoes
2 tablespoonsful vegetable oil
2 oz (50g) polyunsaturated margarine
1 teaspoonful basil or marjoram
1½ lb (¾ kilo) mashed potatoes (made up from that
  amount of fresh potatoes plus plant milk,
  polyunsaturated margarine, sea salt and freshly ground
  black pepper, or from Barbara's Organic Mashed Potatoes
  – 4 portions)

1. Chop the onions finely and *sauté* them in the oil and
   margarine for 3 or 4 minutes.

2. Mince the celery (if used), chop the tomatoes and slice the
   mushrooms. Add these to the onions.

3. Stir well over a moderate heat for 2 or 3 minutes. Add the
   herbs. Lower the heat, cover the saucepan, and simmer for
   about 10 minutes.

4. Place the mixture in a baking dish and cover with mashed
   potatoes. Bake for about 30 minutes in a moderately hot
   oven at 375°F/190°C (Gas Mark 5) until golden brown on
   top. Alternatively, if the ingredients have all been kept hot,
   place under the grill until browned.

SMOKEY LEEK PASTIES

½lb (¼ kilo) wholemeal pastry (see p. 11)
½oz (15g) polyunsaturated margarine
½oz (15g) wholemeal flour
¼ pint (150ml) soya milk
½ teaspoonful sage
3 medium-sized leeks
1-2 tablespoonsful Smokey Snaps
Sea salt to taste

1. Heat the margarine in a small saucepan and add the flour. Add the soya milk carefully, stirring constantly to avoid lumps.

2. Chop the leeks and blanch them in boiling water for 3 minutes then drain them well.

3. Roll out the pastry and cut into 4 rounds with a saucer.

4. Mix the leeks, Smokey Snaps and sage with the white sauce. Season to taste.

5. Spoon the mixture onto the centre of the pastry circles. Bring the edges up to meet on top and pinch well together all round.

6. Bake in a hot oven at 425°F/220°C (Gas Mark 7) for 10 minutes, then lower the heat to moderate 350°F/180°C (Gas Mark 4) and cook for a further 20-30 minutes until the pastry is well cooked.

POTATO KEPHTIDES

1 lb (½ kilo) cold boiled potatoes
½ oz (15g) polyunsaturated margarine
2 spring onions
2 large tomatoes
2 oz (50g) wholemeal flour
Sea salt and freshly ground black pepper to taste
Vegetable oil for frying

1. Chop the spring onions finely, peel and chop the tomatoes and melt the margarine.

2. Sieve the potatoes and mix them with all the other ingredients. Knead slightly and roll out ¾ inch thick. Cut into rounds about 2½ inches across.

3. Heat the oil until smoking hot and fry quickly. Alternatively, they can be baked on a greased baking sheet in a hot oven at 425°F/220°C (Gas Mark 7) until golden brown. They should be crisp outside but very soft inside.

AUBERGINE AU GRATIN

1½-2 lb (¾-1 kilo) aubergines
4 squares Shredded Wheat
2 onions
Sea salt to taste
4 tablespoonsful vegetable oil
1 medium-sized tin tomatoes
2 tablespoonsful tomato *purée*
2 teaspoonsful basil or marjoram

1. Chop the onion and *sauté* it for 2-3 minutes in the oil, adding the crushed Shredded Wheat. *Sauté*, stirring well, until slightly browned. Season with salt.

2. Slice the aubergines. Place alternate layers of aubergine and browned mixture in a greased baking dish.

3. Liquidize the tinned tomatoes, tomato *purée* and herbs and pour this over the layers.

4. Bake in a moderately hot oven at 375°F/190°C (Gas Mark 5) for 45 minutes-1 hour, until the aubergine is tender when tested with a fork.

CURRIED VEGETABLE RING

3 oz (75 g) polyunsaturated margarine
8 onions
1 Bramley apple
3 teaspoonsful curry powder
1 dessertspoonful wholemeal flour
1 pint (½ litre) vegetable stock
1 tablespoonful mango chutney
1 dessertspoonful tomato ketchup
1 tablespoonful raisins
12 oz (350 g) carrots
2 oz (50 g) turnips
¼ cucumber
6 oz (200 g) mushrooms
2 lb (1 kilo) mashed potatoes

1. Chop the onions finely and peel and chop the apple.

2. Melt 1 oz (25 g) polyunsaturated margarine and fry the onions and apple until soft.

3. Add the curry powder and fry for a further minute. Add the flour and stir well. Add the vegetable stock, stirring constantly to avoid lumps. Bring to the boil, and boil for 1 minute, stirring.

4. Add the chutney, ketchup and raisins, cover and simmer while preparing the vegetables.

5. Chop the carrots, turnips, cucumber and mushrooms. Melt the remaining margarine and fry the vegetables until golden.

6. Add the vegetables to the curry sauce and simmer gently for about 20-30 minutes.

7. Make a mashed potato border on a hot dish and pour the curried vegetables into the centre.

STUFFED GREEN PEPPERS

4 green peppers
1 medium-sized onion
2 large tomatoes
3 tablespoonsful polyunsaturated margarine
1 medium-sized tin creamed-style sweet corn
1 teaspoonful sea salt
2 oz (50g) wholemeal breadcrumbs

1. Cut a slice from the stem end of the green peppers and scoop out the seeds and dividing membranes. Parboil for about 2 minutes in boiling water then drain thoroughly.

2. Chop the onion, peel and chop the tomatoes and *sauté* both in 2 tablespoonsful of the margarine until softened.

3. Add the creamed-style sweet corn and salt, and heat to bubbling.

4. Stuff the mixture into the parboiled pepper cases.

5. Melt the remaining tablespoonsful of margarine and toss the breadcrumbs in this.

6. Sprinkle the breadcrumbs over the peppers and place them in an oiled shallow baking dish.

7. Bake in a fairly hot oven at 400°F/200°C (Gas Mark 6) for about 30 minutes, until the peppers are tender.

POTATO-PAPRIKA

4 tablespoonsful vegetable oil
3 onions
1 green pepper
1 red pepper
8 large cooked potatoes
⅓ pint (200ml) soya yogurt (see p. 20)
2 dessertspoonsful paprika
Sea salt to taste
Sprinkling of caraway seeds (optional)

1. Chop the onions and slice the peppers into thin slivers.

2. *Sauté* the onions in the oil until beginning to brown, then add the peppers.

3. Cube the cooked potatoes and add these to the pan. Sprinkle with paprika, salt and seeds (if used). Fry lightly, stirring well.

4. Pour on the soya yogurt, heat through without bringing to the boil, and serve.

CREOLE-STYLE AUBERGINE

1-1½ lbs (½-¾ kilo) aubergines
3 oz (75g) polyunsaturated margarine
2 oz (50g) wholemeal flour
1½ lb (¾ kilo) ripe tomatoes
2 small green peppers
2 small onions
1 teaspoonful sea salt
1 dessertspoonful raw cane sugar
1 bay leaf
3 cloves
2 oz (50g) wholemeal breadcrumbs

1. Peel and dice the aubergines. Cook for 10 minutes in boiling water then drain well and place in an oiled baking dish.

2. Melt 2 oz (50 g) of the margarine and stir in the flour.

3. Peel and slice the tomatoes, chop the green peppers and onions and add these to the saucepan, stirring well.

4. Add the salt, sugar, bay leaf and cloves and cook for 5 minutes.

5. Pour the mixture over the aubergines. Cover with the breadcrumbs and top with the rest of the margarine.

6. Bake in a moderate oven at 350°F/180°C (Gas Mark 4) for 30 minutes.

CABBAGE AND POTATO CASSEROLE

1 lb (½ kilo) cooked potatoes
1 lb (½ kilo) cooked cabbage
2 tablespoonsful (or more to taste) Smokey Snaps
1 oz (25 g) polyunsaturated margarine
Soya milk as required

1. Slice the potatoes and put a layer in the bottom of an oiled baking dish.

2. Sprinkle with Smokey Snaps.

3. Chop the cabbage and place a layer in the baking dish.

4. Repeat the layers until the ingredients have all been used up, finishing with potato.

5. Pour over enough soya milk to moisten and dot with margarine.

6. Bake in a moderately hot oven at 375°F/190°C (Gas Mark 5) for 30 minutes.

TOMATO AND SWEET CORN SAVOURY

1 medium-sized onion
2 tablespoonful vegetable oil
1 small green pepper
1 medium-sized tin sweet corn
4 large tomatoes
2 tablespoonful cornflour
½ pint (¼ litre) water
½ teaspoonful garlic salt
3 tablespoonful Smokey Snaps

1. Chop the onion and green pepper finely.

2. *Sauté* them in the vegetable oil until beginning to soften.

3. Chop the tomatoes and add them to the saucepan. Add the sweet corn and *sauté* for a few more minutes, stirring well.

4. Dissolve the cornflour in a little water, add the rest of the water, mix well and add to the saucepan. Bring to the boil, stirring constantly.

5. Add the garlic salt and Smokey Snaps and simmer for a few more minutes.

Note: This dish may be served over brown rice or other grains, or with potatoes.

7.
NUT-BASED SAVOURIES

CASHEW NUT ROAST

½ lb (¼ kilo) cashew nuts
4 oz (100g) short grain brown rice
4 oz (100g) fresh wholemeal breadcrumbs
1 medium-sized onion
2 cloves garlic
4 tablespoonsful vegetable oil
2 teaspoonsful yeast extract
1 teaspoonful mixed herbs
Sea salt and freshly ground black pepper to taste

1. Cook the brown rice until tender and grind the cashew nuts.

2. Chop the onion and garlic finely and fry them in the vegetable oil until browned.

3. Combine all the ingredients and press the mixture into a loaf tin.

4. Bake for 30 minutes in a moderate oven at 350°F/180°C (Gas Mark 4).

NUT CRUNCH AND MUSHROOM CREAM

4 oz (100g) wholemeal breadcrumbs
2 oz (50g) ground almonds
1-2 cloves garlic
4 oz (100g) polyunsaturated margarine
1 teaspoonful mixed herbs
4 oz (100g) chopped or flaked almonds
12 oz (350g) mushrooms
1 oz (25g) wholemeal flour
½ pint (¼ litre) soya milk
2 tomatoes
Sea salt, freshly ground black pepper and grated nutmeg
  to taste

1. Combine the crumbs and ground almonds. Crush the garlic and add it to the nuts.

2. Rub half the margarine into this mixture, then stir in the mixed herbs and chopped almonds.

3. Turn the mixture into a greased ovenproof dish. Press down firmly and bake in a hot oven at 425°F/220°C (Gas Mark 7) until lightly browned and crisp.

4. Slice the mushrooms and *sauté* them in the remainder of the margarine until tender.

5. Add the flour and stir well. Then add the soya milk slowly, stirring constantly to avoid lumps. Bring to the boil and simmer for 2 minutes. Season to taste.

6. Spoon the mixture on top of the breadcrumb and nut base and spread evenly.

7. Slice the tomatoes and arrange them on the top.

8. Return the dish to the oven for 10-15 minutes and serve hot.

CASHEW-STUFFED AUBERGINES

2 large or 4 small aubergines
1 lb (½ kilo) onions
½ lb (¼ kilo) cashew nuts
1 dessertspoonful yeast extract

1. Cut the tops off the aubergines and simmer them in boiling water for half an hour. Set them aside to drain and cool.

2. Chop the onions finely and cook them in enough water to cover, along with the yeast extract, until tender. Drain the surplus liquid.

3. Grind the cashews and mix them with the cooked onions.

4. Slice the aubergines in half, remove the centres and, when finely chopped, add them to the cashew-onion mixture.

5. Pile the mixture onto the aubergine halves and bake for 20 minutes in a fairly hot oven at 400°F/200°C (Gas Mark 6) for 20 minutes.

SHEPHERD'S PIE

3 tablespoonsful vegetable oil
2 onions
2 tomatoes
1 large carrot
½lb (¼ kilo) mushrooms
2oz (50g) hazelnuts
2 tablespoonsful rissole mix (from health food stores)
1oz (25g) wholemeal flour
½ cupful (150ml) water
1 dessertspoonful yeast extract
Mashed potatoes (made up from 1lb (½ kilo) fresh
  potatoes, soya milk and polyunsaturated margarine, or 4
  portions of Barbara's Organic Mashed Potatoes)

1. Chop the onions and *sauté* them until tender.

2. Grate the carrot and chop the tomatoes and mushrooms. Add them to the saucepan and *sauté* until the mushrooms are tender.

3. Stir in the yeast extract and wholemeal flour for a minute or two. Add the water slowly, stirring constantly to avoid lumps.

4. Grind the hazelnuts and add them to the saucepan along with the rissole mix.

5. Place the mixture in a casserole, cover with the mashed potato, and brown under the grill.

SAVOURY NUT ROAST

1 onion
3 tablespoonsful vegetable oil
2 small tomatoes
1 oz (25 g) wholemeal flour
¼ pint (150 ml) water
1 tablespoonful soya sauce
4 oz (100 g) hazelnuts
4 oz (100 g) broken cashew nuts
3 oz (75 g) fresh wholemeal breadcrumbs
1 teaspoonful mixed herbs
1 oz (25 g) soya flour

1. Chop the onion finely and *sauté* it in the oil until tender.

2. Skin and chop the tomatoes and add them to the pan. Cook for 5 minutes.

3. Stir in the flour and slowly add the water, stirring constantly to avoid lumps. Remove from the heat.

4. Grind the hazelnuts and add them to the sauce along with all the other ingredients. Mix very thoroughly and place in a bread tin or pie dish.

5. Bake in a moderate oven at 350°F/180°C (Gas Mark 4) for 45 minutes-1 hour.

NUT CROQUETTES

½ lb (¼ kilo) mixed nuts
1 oz (25g) vegetable fat or polyunsaturated margarine
2 oz (50g) wholemeal flour
½ pint (¼ litre) soya milk
1 small onion
1 teaspoonful lemon juice
1 teaspoonful mixed herbs
Sea salt and freshly ground black pepper to taste
Vegetable oil for frying

1. Chop the nuts very finely and mince or grate the onion.

2. Melt the fat, stir in the flour, then add the soya milk, stirring constantly to avoid lumps.

3. When thickened, add all the other ingredients, seasoning to taste.

4. Leave the mixture to cool, then form into croquette shapes.

5. Deep fry them in hot oil, 350°F/180°C until brown.

CURRIED CASHEWS

10 oz (300 g) whole cashews
1 small onion
1 clove garlic
Small piece fresh ginger
1 fresh chilli
1 teaspoonful turmeric
1 cinnamon stick
2 cardamom pods
Grated rind of ½ lemon
Sea salt to taste
⅓ pint (200 ml) water
1 oz (25 g) creamed coconut

1. Mince the onion and chilli finely, making certain the chilli seeds have been discarded. Crush the garlic and grate the ginger.

2. Combine these ingredients with all of the spices and cover them with the water. Simmer for a few minutes.

3. Add the cashews and creamed coconut, and simmer for a further 20-30 minutes. Serve over brown rice.

SAVOURY STUFFED AUBERGINES

2 large or 4 small aubergines
1 onion
2 large tomatoes
3 oz (75g) almonds, Brazils or hazelnuts
1 clove garlic
4 tablespoonsful porridge oats
4 tablespoonsful vegetable oil
2 tablespoonsful wholemeal flour
1 medium-sized tin tomatoes
1 teaspoonful basil or marjoram
Sea salt and freshly ground black pepper to taste

1. Cut the tops off the aubergines and place them in boiling water for 5-10 minutes.

2. Set aside to drain, then slice them in half and remove the flesh, leaving the skins intact.

3. Mince the garlic finely. Chop the onion, the 2 large tomatoes, and the aubergine flesh.

4. *Sauté* the above ingredients in half the oil for a few minutes.

5. Grind the nuts and add them to the saucepan along with the oats, stirring well.

6. Fill the aubergine skins with this mixture and bake them in a moderately hot oven at 375°F/190°C (Gas Mark 5) for about 30 minutes.

7. Meanwhile, heat the rest of the oil in a small saucepan and stir in the flour. Remove from the heat.

8. Pour the whole tin of tomatoes into the liquidizer and blend them thoroughly. Add this to the saucepan, mixing well. Return to the heat, stirring constantly to avoid lumps. When thickened and boiling, add the herbs and seasoning to taste.

9. Pour this tomato sauce over the aubergines when ready to serve.

HAZELNUT SAVOURY

6 oz (200g) hazelnuts
2 stalks celery
3 spring onions
1 teaspoonful garlic salt
12 oz (350g) mashed potatoes (made from either that
  quantity of fresh potatoes or 3 servings of Barbara's
  Organic Mashed Potatoes)
1 oz (25g) polyunsaturated margarine
1 oz (25g) wholemeal flour
¼ pint (150ml) soya milk

1. Grind the nuts and mince the celery and spring onions finely.

2. Combine these ingredients with the mashed potatoes and garlic salt.

3. Melt the margarine in a small saucepan and stir in the flour. Slowly add the soya milk, stirring constantly to avoid lumps. When boiling and thickened, combine this sauce with the mashed potato-nut mixture.

4. Place the mixture in a baking dish and bake in a moderate oven at 350°F/180°C (Gas Mark 4) for 30 minutes.

STEAMED NUT SAVOURY

2 onions
2 tablespoonsful vegetable oil
2 tablespoonsful wholemeal flour
1 teaspoonful thyme
3 tablespoonsful soya flour
2 teaspoonsful yeast extract
¼ pint (150 ml) water
6 oz (200 g) Brazil nuts
2 oz (50 g) broken cashew nuts
4 oz (100 g) wholemeal breadcrumbs

1. Chop the onions finely and *sauté* them in the oil until brown.

2. Add the flour. Slowly add the water, stirring constantly to avoid lumps, and then add the yeast extract. When the sauce has boiled and thickened, remove the pan from the heat.

3. Grind the Brazils, and add them to the mixture along with the broken cashews, soya flour, breadcrumbs and thyme. Mix well.

4. Turn into a pudding basin, cover with tin foil and steam for 1½-2 hours.

8.
PROPRIETARY HEALTH FOOD PRODUCTS

POTATO AND NUTMEAT CASSEROLE

2 lb (1 kilo) potatoes
1 large tin nut savoury (e.g. Mapletons Luncheon Roll,
  Granose Protose, Nut Loaf, Nuttolene etc.)
⅓ pint (200 ml) soya milk
1 small onion
2 tablespoonsful vegetable oil
½ teaspoonful sage or marjoram
2 tablespoonsful wholemeal flour
Sea salt to taste

1. Cook the potatoes until tender, drain, cool and dice them
   and set aside.

2. Chop the onion finely and *sauté* it in the oil until tender.

3. Add the wholemeal flour and stir well for 1-2 minutes.
   Slowly add the soya milk, stirring constantly to prevent
   lumps. Bring to the boil and add the herbs and salt.

4. Dice the nut savoury and add it to the soya milk mixture
   along with the potatoes.

5. Place the whole mixture in an oiled casserole and bake for
   approximately 30 minutes in a moderate oven at
   350°F/180°C (Gas Mark 4).

QUICK SAUSALATA PIE

1 large tin Granose Sausalatas (or make up the equivalent
amount of 'sausages' from Direct Foods Sosmix, Itona
Tonabanga, or any T.V.P. 'sausage' mix)
4 large onions
½ teaspoonful thyme
2 tablespoonsful vegetable oil
1½lb (¾ kilo) mashed potatoes (made up from fresh
potatoes combined with soya milk and polyunsaturated
margarine or from Barbara's Organic Mashed Potatoes – 6
portions)

1. Chop the onions and fry them until tender. Add the
    Sausalatas or made-up 'sausages' and fry them with the
    onions until everything is browned.

2. Place in an oiled pie dish, sprinkle with thyme and cover
    with mashed potatoes.

3. Bake in a moderate oven at 350°F/180°C (Gas Mark 4) until
    the top is golden brown, or if the ingredients have been kept
    warm, place under the grill instead.

SAUSALATA AND MACARONI CASSEROLE

1 large tin Granose Sausalatas (or make up the equivalent
  any of the 'sausage' mixes mentioned in the recipe above)
2 medium-sized onions
1 small green pepper
2 medium-sized tins tomatoes
½ pint (¼ litre) soya yogurt (see p. 20)
2 tablespoonsful vegetable oil
1 teaspoonful mixed herbs
1 teaspoonful raw cane sugar
Cayenne pepper to taste
½ lb (¼ kilo) wholemeal macaroni

1. Cook the macaroni until tender in boiling salted water. Set
    aside to drain.

2. Chop the onion and green pepper and fry them in the
    vegetable oil until tender.

3. Mash the Sausalatas (or add the made-up 'sausage' mix
    direct) and add it to saucepan.

4. Liquidize the tomatoes and add them to the saucepan along
    with mixed herbs, sugar, cayenne pepper, and soya yogurt.
    Cook for several minutes on a very low heat until thoroughly
    heated and cooked.

5. Add the macaroni, stir well, and cook for another 2-3
    minutes and serve.

NUTMEAT STEW

2 onions
4 oz (100g) mushrooms
1 medium-sized tin tomatoes
1 bay leaf
1 medium-sized tin nut savoury (as in first recipe)
1 teaspoonful garlic salt
1 tablespoonful polyunsaturated margarine

1. Chop the onion, slice the mushrooms, and fry them gently
    in the margarine with the bay leaf for 10 minutes.

2. Add the tinned tomatoes, garlic salt and diced nut savoury
    and cook for several minutes more on a gentle heat before
    serving.

SWEET AND SOUR NUTMEAT

1 medium-sized tin nut savoury (as in first recipe)
2 tablespoonsful (or more if required) vegetable oil
4 teaspoonsful cornflour
1 tablespoonful soya sauce
1 tablespoonful cider vinegar
1 tablespoonful raw cane sugar
1 small tin pineapple chunks
1 small onion
½ pint (¼ litre) vegetable stock or water
½ teaspoonful ginger

1. Dice the nut savoury and fry the cubes in the oil until
    browned and crisp.

2. Grate the onion, combine it with the soya sauce, vinegar,
    sugar and stock and heat gently.

3. Mix the cornflour with a little water and add it to the saucepan. Stir until mixture thickens.

4. Drain the pineapple and add this to the saucepan. Stir until heated, then pour the mixture over the nut savoury cubes. This may then be served over brown rice or other grains.

SAVOURY STUFFED PANCAKES

6oz (200g) finely ground wholemeal flour (or 81 per cent, if preferred)
3 tablespoonsful soya flour
1 teaspoonful baking powder
2 teaspoonsful vegetable oil
1 teaspoonful sea salt
Water as required
2 small or 1 large tin vegetable pâté (e.g. Tartex or Granose)
1 tablespoonful undiluted soya milk
4 large tomatoes
Polyunsaturated margarine or vegetable oil for frying

1. Combine the flour, soya flour, baking powder and sea salt. Make a well in the centre, pour in the oil, then pour in the water gradually, stirring constantly with a fork. The consistency should be like thick cream. Leave to stand for 30 minutes. If it is too thick then add more water, if too thin, add more flour.

2. Beat the pâté with the undiluted soya milk.

3. Chop the tomatoes roughly.

4. Heat the margarine or oil, pour in a little batter at a time and fry on both sides.

5. Fill each pancake with a little pâté and some of the chopped tomato.

LASAGNE BOLOGNESE

1 large tin nut savoury (as in first recipe)
1 medium-sized onion
1 medium-sized carrot
1 stalk celery
1 tin tomato *purée*
1 medium-sized tin tomatoes
½ lb (¼ kilo) wholemeal lasagne
Soya 'cheese' (see p. 21) made up from 4 oz (100g)
  polyunsaturated margarine, etc.
1 pint (½ litre) soya milk
2 oz (50g) polyunsaturated margarine
1 oz (25g) cornflour
Pinch of dry mustard
Sea salt and freshly ground black pepper to taste

1. Cook the lasagne in boiling salted water for about 15-20 minutes until tender. Set aside to drain.

2. Chop the onion, carrot and celery and fry them in the vegetable oil until tender.

3. Mash the nut savoury and add it to the saucepan along with the tomato *purée* and tinned tomatoes. Cover the pan and simmer for a few minutes.

4. Heat the margarine in a small saucepan. Add the cornflour, then slowly add the soya milk, stirring constantly to avoid lumps. When thickened, add mustard, salt and pepper as well as about three-quarters of the soya 'cheese'. Continue stirring over a gentle heat until well blended.

5. In an oiled casserole, layer a third of the lasagne, top with half the nutmeat sauce and a third of the 'cheese' sauce. Repeat and top the third layer of lasagne with the remainder of the 'cheese' sauce and cover with the remainder of the soya 'cheese', grated or cut into small pieces.

6. Bake in a fairly hot oven at 400°F/200°C (Gas Mark 6) for 30 minutes.

CAULIFLOWER À LA CRÈME

1 very large cauliflower
Sea salt to taste
2 small or 1 large tin vegetable pâté (e.g. Granose or Tartex)
⅓ pint (200 ml) undiluted plant milk or double concentration Granogen
Sprinkling of paprika

1. Remove the outside leaves from the cauliflower, leaving the tender ones round the sides, and wash it thoroughly.

2. Place the cauliflower, stalk side down, in a large saucepan of boiling salted water. Cover and simmer gently until tender.

3. Heat the concentrated soya milk and pâté together, stirring well to avoid lumps.

4. Drain the cauliflower, pour the sauce over it and dust with paprika.

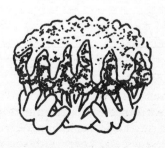

9.
VEGETABLE SIDE DISHES

CABBAGE, CARROTS AND APPLE

1 medium-sized cabbage
2 large carrots
2 dessert apples
1 oz (25g) polyunsaturated margarine

1. Shred the cabbage, grate the carrots, and dice the apples.

2. Melt the margarine, add the cabbage and cook for 2-3 minutes, stirring well.

3. Add the carrots and apples, lower the heat, cover the pan tightly, and simmer until just tender.

MUSHROOMS AND CELERY

2 small heads or 1 large head celery
½lb (¼ kilo) mushrooms
1½oz (40g) polyunsaturated margarine
1 dessertspoonful wholemeal flour
¼ pint (150ml) soya milk
Sea salt and finely ground black pepper to taste

1. Slice the celery into 2-inch pieces and cook until tender in salted water.

2. Prepare and slice the mushrooms into halves or quarters, depending on the size.

3. Melt the margarine, add the mushrooms and stir well.

4. Sprinkle the flour into the mixture, stirring again.

5. Add the drained celery pieces, stir in the soya milk carefully and mix well. Add seasoning to taste.

6. Cook gently for 4-5 minutes and serve.

SAVOURY FRIED CABBAGE

1lb (½ kilo) cabbage
1 onion
1 clove garlic
2 teaspoonsful soya sauce (or more to taste)
1 teaspoonful cornflour
2 tablespoonsful water
2 tablespoonsful vegetable oil

1. Shred the cabbage and chop the onion and garlic finely.

2. Heat the oil in a heavy frying pan, add the onion and garlic and *sauté* until beginning to soften.

3. Add the cabbage, increase the heat and stir constantly for 3-6 minutes.

4. Combine the cornflour, water and soya sauce in a small cup. Pour this mixture over the vegetables in the frying pan, stir well until thoroughly mixed and thickened and serve.

BROCCOLI WITH ALMONDS, ONIONS AND GARLIC

2 lb (1 kilo) broccoli
3 fl oz (80 ml) vegetable oil
1½ oz (40 g) blanched almonds
2 cloves garlic
1 small onion
3 tablespoonsful capers
Sea salt and freshly ground black pepper to taste

1. Prepare the broccoli and cook it in lightly salted water until just tender. Set aside to drain well.

2. Slice the almonds, chop the onion and mince the garlic.

3. *Sauté* the onion, garlic and almonds in oil until browned.

4. Add the broccoli, capers and seasoning to the pan and cook over a high heat for 1 minute, stirring well, and serve.

CAULIFLOWER ROMAGNA-STYLE

1 medium-sized cauliflower
1 oz (25 g) polyunsaturated margarine
3 tablespoonsful vegetable oil
1 clove garlic
2 tablespoonsful chopped parsley
Sea salt and freshly ground black pepper to taste
6 tablespoonsful water
1 tablespoonful tomato *purée*

1. Divide the washed cauliflower into individual florets and crush the garlic.

2. Heat the margarine and oil in a saucepan and fry the garlic and parsley for a few moments.

3. Add the cauliflower, stir and cook for several minutes, then add the seasoning, water and tomato *purée*. Cover the pan and cook over a low heat until tender (about 20-25 minutes).

RUNNER BEANS À LA GRECQUE

1 lb (½ kilo) runner beans
1 tin tomato *purée*
1 pint (½ litre) water
4 tablespoonsful vegetable oil
1 small onion
1 small clove garlic
Sea salt and freshly ground black pepper to taste

1. Slice the runner beans and mince the onion and garlic.

2. Mix the tomato *purée* with the water, oil, onion and garlic.

3. Put the beans in a saucepan and pour over them the tomato-onion mixture. Season to taste.

4. Bring to the boil then lower the heat and simmer gently, stirring from time to time, for half an hour or until the sauce has reduced and the beans are tender.

BAKED TOMATOES WITH POTATOES

1lb (½ kilo) potatoes
1½lb (¾ kilo) tomatoes
2 cloves garlic
1 dessertspoonful oregano or thyme
½ pint (¼ litre) undiluted tinned soya milk or Granogen
    made up at double strength
½oz (15g) polyunsaturated margarine
Sea salt and freshly ground black pepper to taste
2 tablespoonsful chopped parsley

1.   Boil the potatoes in salted water until tender and peel them, if desired.

2.   Pour boiling water over the tomatoes and then peel them. Slice the potatoes and tomatoes into fairly thick slices.

3.   In a casserole, place a layer of potatoes, a little crushed garlic, a dot or two of the margarine, a sprinkling of salt and pepper, a layer of tomatoes, a sprinkling of herbs, and so on until the ingredients are used up, ending with a layer of tomatoes.

4.   Pour the concentrated soya milk over the vegetables.

5.   Cover the dish and cook in the centre of a moderate oven at 350°F/180°C (Gas Mark 4) for half an hour. Before serving, sprinkle some chopped parsley over the top.

SAUCE FOR VEGETABLES

1½oz (40g) polyunsaturated margarine
3 tablespoonsful wholemeal flour
Dash of freshly ground black pepper
⅓ pint (200ml) soya yogurt (see p. 20)
3 tablespoonsful soya sauce
4 fl oz (100ml) Sun-O-Life dressing
Dash of paprika
Lightly cooked green beans, cabbage, Brussels sprouts or
  broccoli

1. Melt the margarine in a small saucepan over the lowest
   possible heat. Add the flour and pepper.

2. Stir in the soya yogurt and soya sauce. Continue stirring
   constantly to avoid lumps until the sauce thickens.

3. Gently stir in the Sun-O-Life dressing and continue cooking
   briefly until heated through.

4. Pour the sauce over the vegetables and garnish with paprika.

10.
CAKES AND DESSERTS

CHRISTMAS CAKE

3 oz (75g) Trex vegetable fat or nut fat (from health food
   stores)
4 oz (100g) raw cane sugar
Juice of 2 small oranges
4 oz (100g) 81 per cent wholemeal flour
1 tablespoonful mixed spice
1 lb (½ kilo) mixed dried fruit

1. Cream the fat and sugar together.

2. Add the rest of the ingredients and mix thoroughly.

3. Bake in a tin lined with greased greaseproof paper for 3
    hours in a slow oven at 300°F/150°C (Gas Mark 2).

4. Allow to cool completely. This can be stored for several
    weeks in a cool place, covered with greaseproof paper and
    then foil. If desired, top with marzipan made from a mixture
    of ground almonds, soya flour, lemon juice and almond
    extract, and ice with a white *glacé* icing.

ORANGE CAKE

4 oz (100g) raw cane sugar
½ teaspoonful sea salt
7 oz (200g) 81 per cent or 100 per cent plain wholemeal
  flour
1 teaspoonful bicarbonate of soda
4 tablespoonsful vegetable oil
2 tablespoonsful pure orange juice
Grated rind of 1 small orange
⅓ pint (200ml) water

1. Mix the flour, sugar, salt and soda together well in a large
    bowl.

2. Add the oil, juice, rind and water. Mix with a fork until all the
    dry ingredients are moist. Do not beat.

3. Pour the mixture into two greased (and, if desired, lined
    with greaseproof paper) sandwich tins.

4. Bake in a moderate oven at 350°F/180°C (Gas Mark 4) for 30
    minutes, or until the top of the cake springs up when lightly
    pressed. Leave to cool thoroughly.

Note: This cake is nice sandwiched with margarine mixed with
raw cane sugar and pure orange juice and topped with an
orange-flavoured *glacé* icing.

PLAIN SPONGE CAKE

½ pint (¼ litre) soya milk
4 tablespoonsful vegetable oil
9 oz (250g) 81 per cent or 100 per cent plain wholemeal
flour
4 oz (100g) raw cane sugar
3 teaspoonsful baking powder
½ teaspoonful sea salt
2 teaspoonsful vanilla essence

1. Pour the soya milk and oil into a mixing bowl. Add the
    vanilla essence.

2. Mix the dry ingredients separately, then add them to the
    liquid ingredients.

3. Stir until thoroughly mixed and pour into two sandwich
    tins.

4. Bake in a fairly hot oven at 400°F/200°C (Gas Mark 6) for
    20-25 minutes or until the top of the cake springs up when
    lightly pressed. Leave to cool thoroughly.

Note: This cake may be sandwiched with margarine mixed with
raw cane sugar and iced, if desired, with Caramel Icing (see
recipe below).

CARAMEL ICING

5 oz (150g) raw cane sugar
4 tablespoonsful soya milk
2 oz (50g) polyunsaturated margarine
½ teaspoonful vanilla essence

1. Mix the sugar, soya milk and margarine in a saucepan.

2. Bring to the boil, stirring constantly. Boil for 2-3 minutes.

3. Remove from the heat and beat until lukewarm.

4. Add the vanilla essence and beat to a spreading consistency.

CHOCOLATE CAKE

4 oz (100g) raw cane sugar
2 dessertspoonsful cocoa or carob powder
½ teaspoonful sea salt
6 oz (200g) 81 per cent or 100 per cent wholemeal flour
¾ teaspoonful bicarbonate of soda
3 fl oz (80ml) vegetable oil
1 teaspoonful vanilla essence
1 dessertspoonful cider vinegar
⅓ pint (200ml) cold water

1. Mix the sugar, cocoa (or carob), salt, flour and bicarbonate of soda well in a mixing bowl.

2. Add the oil, vanilla essence and vinegar and pour cold water over the mixture.

3. Combine well with a fork, but do not beat.

4. Pour into two greased sandwich tins (lined if desired) and bake in a moderate oven at 350°F/180°C (Gas Mark 4) for 30 minutes or until the cake springs back when lightly pressed. Leave to cool thoroughly.

Note: This cake may be iced with Chocolate Icing, if desired (see recipe below).

CHOCOLATE ICING

2 oz (50g) polyunsaturated margarine
1 oz (25g) cocoa or carob powder
4 tablespoonsful soya milk
5 oz (150g) raw cane sugar
1 teaspoonful vanilla essence

1. Combine the first four ingredients in a saucepan and bring them to the boil slowly, stirring constantly.

2. Boil for 1 minute.

3. Remove from the heat and beat until cool. Add the vanilla essence and spread the icing on the cake.

Sweets Without Sugar

RAISIN AND PECAN ICE CREAM

⅓ pint (200ml) pineapple or orange juice
6 oz (200g) raisins
4 oz (100g) pecans
2 large bananas
4 peaches or ½ pineapple

1. Chop the peaches or pineapple and bananas and place the pieces in the freezing compartment of the fridge until frozen.

2. Pour the juice into the liquidizer, add the raisins and pecans and blend thoroughly.

3. Add the frozen fruit, a little at a time, blending thoroughly after each addition. Serve immediately.

CAROB PUDDING

½ pint (¼ litre) water
1 oz (25 g) soya flour
3 oz (75 g) sunflower seeds
4 tablespoonsful carob powder
3 oz (75 g) pitted dates
2 teaspoonsfui vanilla essence

1. Place all the ingredients in the liquidizer and blend thoroughly.

BAKED DATE AND COCONUT PUDDING

12 oz (350g) stoned dates
3 oz (75 g) shredded coconut
4 oz (100g) creamed coconut
1 teaspoonful agar-agar
½ pint (¼ litre) boiling water

1. Chop the dates finely. In an oiled casserole, place alternate layers of chopped dates and shredded coconut.

2. Grate or finely chop the creamed coconut and put it in a liquidizer with the agar-agar. Pour in the boiling water and blend thoroughly.

3. Pour the liquid over the dates and coconut.

4. Bake in a slow oven at 300°F/150°C (Gas Mark 2) for about 30 minutes or until brown on top. Serve hot.

BANANA CREAM PIE

1 pre-baked pastry shell
4 oz (100g) cashew nuts
6 oz (200g) stoned dates
2 dessertspoonsful arrowroot
Pinch of sea salt
1 teaspoonful vanilla essence
½ pint (¼ litre) water
2 ripe bananas

1. Chop the dates and place them in a liquidizer along with the cashews, arrowroot, salt, vanilla and water. Liquidize thoroughly.

2. Pour into a saucepan and heat gently, stirring constantly, until thickened. Allow the mixture to cool.

3. Slice the bananas into the pie shell. Cover them with the cashew-date mixture and serve.

CAROB AND DATE ICE CREAM

4 tablespoonsful vegetable oil
¾ pint (400ml) water
6 oz (200g) stoned dates
1 oz (25g) carob powder
3 oz (75g) Granogen powder
2 teaspoonsful vanilla essence

1. Liquidize the ingredients thoroughly and place the mixture in the freezing compartment of the fridge for at least 3 hours.

Note: This recipe is not 100 per cent sugar-free as Granogen (like all commercial plant milks) does contain some sugar.

CREAMY DATE PUDDING

6 oz (200g) stoned dates
1 teaspoonful vanilla essence
4 oz (100g) creamed coconut
½ pint (¼ litre) hot water

1. Grate or chop the creamed coconut finely and add it to the hot water in a saucepan.

2. Chop the dates and add them to the saucepan.

3. Cook the mixture over the lowest possible heat, stirring occasionally, until the dates have dissolved and the mixture is thick and creamy. Add the vanilla essence.

4. Chill thoroughly before serving.

Sweets With Sugar

FRUIT AND COCONUT ICE CREAM

Juice of 2 lemons
Juice of 2 oranges
2 bananas
6-8 oz (200g-225g) raw cane sugar
1 pint (½ litre) hot water
3 oz (75g) creamed coconut
2 oz (50g) cashew nuts
2 tablespoonsful vegetable oil

1. Grind the cashew nuts finely.

2. Place all of the ingredients in a liquidizer (in stages if necessary) and blend until thoroughly mixed.

3. Freeze in the ice compartment of the fridge at the coldest setting, for at least 2 hours.

STEAMED DATE PUDDING

6 oz (200g) 81 per cent or 100 per cent wholemeal
  self-raising flour
Pinch of sea salt
3 oz (75g) Prova solid vegetable oil or Suenut (from
  health food stores)
1 oz (25g) raw cane sugar
4 oz (100g) dates
¼ pint (150ml) soya milk
Grated rind of 1 lemon (use the juice for a sauce)

1. Chop the dates finely.

2. Grate the fat and mix it in with the flour, salt and sugar. Add the dates and lemon rind.

3. Make a well in the centre and add enough soya milk to give a soft dropping consistency.

4. Place in a greased basin, cover with greased greaseproof paper or foil and steam for 1½-2 hours.

5. Serve with a lemon sauce.

TRIFLE

½ lb (¼ kilo) plain sponge cake (see p. 116)
1 pint (½ litre) soya milk
Custard powder and raw cane sugar as required
1 large tin fruit cocktail
1 Snowcrest fruit jelly

1. Crumble the cake into the bottom of the dish.

2. Pour the tin of fruit cocktail over the cake.

3. Make up the jelly according to the directions on the packet

and pour it over the cake and fruit.

4. Make up a thick custard with the soya milk according to the directions on the packet and when the jelly has set, spread this over the top.

5. Leave in the fridge for several hours before serving.

BAKED RAISIN PUDDING

4 oz (100g) raw cane sugar
1 oz (25g) polyunsaturated margarine
3-4 oz (75-100g) raisins
12 tablespoonsful boiling water
1 teaspoonful vanilla essence
1 oz (25g) chopped nuts
3 oz (75g) 81 per cent or 100 per cent plain wholemeal flour
1 teaspoonful baking powder
Approx. 5 tablespoonsful soya milk

1. First make a syrup by putting half the sugar, half the margarine and the raisins in a small saucepan with the boiling water. Heat slowly until the sugar dissolves, then boil steadily for 10 minutes. Add the vanilla essence.

2. Meanwhile, cream the rest of the sugar and the margarine, add the flour mixed with the baking powder, and stir in enough soya milk to make a thick batter consistency.

3. Turn the mixture into a greased ovenproof dish and pour the hot sauce over the top with a sprinkling of nuts.

4. Bake in a moderate oven at 350°F/180°C (Gas Mark 4) for 30 minutes. Serve immediately.

BLACKCURRANT ICE

1lb (½ kilo) fresh blackcurrants
Juice of 2 lemons
3-4oz (75-100g) raw cane sugar

1. Top and tail the blackcurrants.

2. *Purée* the fruit (in 2 batches if necessary) in a liquidizer.

3. Add the lemon juice to the sugar and stir well. Mix this in with the fruit *purée*.

4. Freeze the mixture in the ice compartment of the fridge. If desired, when almost stiff, *purée* again in a liquidizer just before serving.

STRAWBERRY SHORTCAKE

½lb (¼ kilo) 81 per cent plain wholemeal flour
4 teaspoonsful baking powder
1 teaspoonful sea salt
1 tablespoonful raw cane sugar
1-2oz (25-50g) polyunsaturated margarine
4 floz (100ml) undiluted plant milk with 4 tablespoonsful water or ¼ pint (150ml) water with 1oz (25g) Granogen powder
Mock Cream (p.17) or Soya Whipped Cream (pp.15 and 16) as required
Fresh strawberries as required

1. Mix the flour with the baking powder, salt and sugar.

2. Add the margarine, cut into small pieces, with a pastry blender, two knives, or the fingers, and mix until thoroughly blended. (The larger amount of margarine will make a richer dessert.)

3. Make a well in the centre and pour in the soya milk. Stir it vigorously for the shortest possible time then turn the dough out onto a floured board.

4. Cut the dough in half and roll out each half. Bake in two sandwich tins in a hot oven at 425°F/220°C (Gas Mark 7) for 12-15 minutes.

5. Leave to cool, then sandwich and top the layers with 'cream' and strawberries (sweetened if desired).

STEAMED JAM PUDDING

6 oz (200g) 81 per cent or 100 per cent wholemeal
  self-raising flour
2 oz (50g) soya flour
2 oz (50g) raw cane sugar
3-4 oz (75-100g) polyunsaturated margarine
Soya milk as required
Raw sugar jam as required

1. Mix the flour, sugar and soya flour and rub in the margarine.

2. Add enough soya milk to make a soft dough.

3. Put some raw sugar jam at the bottom of a pudding basin and add the pudding mixture.

4. Cover with greaseproof paper or tin foil and steam for 1 hour.

5. Serve with soya milk custard if desired.

APPLE MOUSSE

1lb (½ kilo) cooking apples
4oz (100g) raw cane sugar
Juice of 1 lemon
½ pint (¼ litre) water
1 teaspoonful agar-agar
3oz (75g) cashew nuts

1. Grind the cashew nuts finely.

2. Peel and slice the apples and cook them with the sugar in just enough of the water to cover. When tender, add the rest of the water and bring to the boil.

3. Sprinkle the agar-agar carefully into the saucepan and cook for 1 minute.

4. Pour the mixture into a liquidizer. Add the lemon juice and ground cashew nuts and blend them thoroughly.

5. Pour into a serving dish or four individual dishes and leave the mousse to cool, then chill before serving.

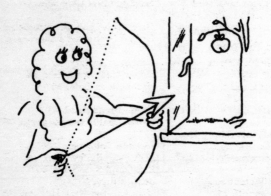

INDEX